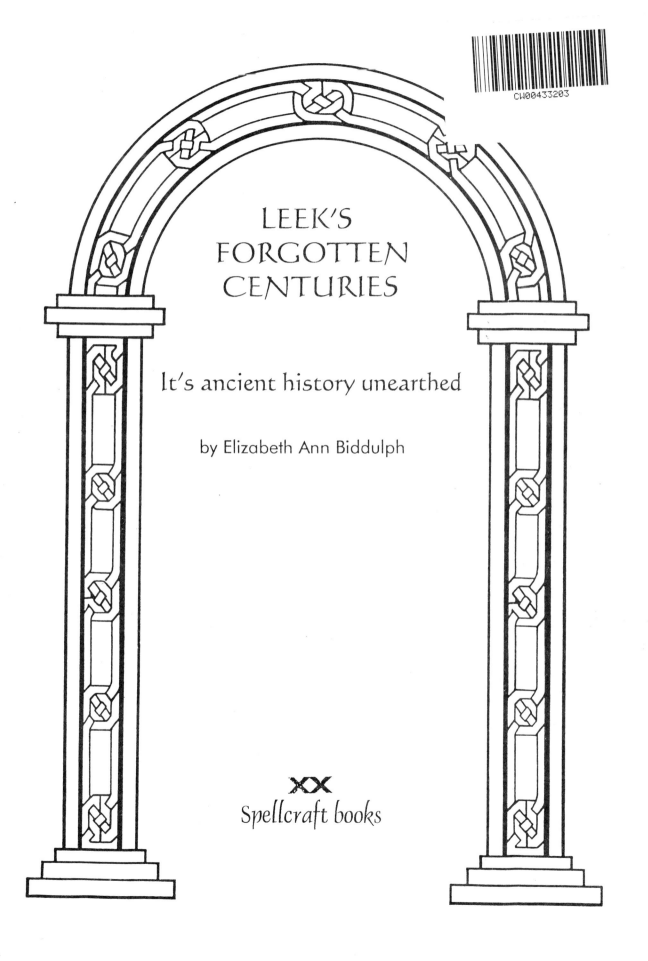

LEEK'S FORGOTTEN CENTURIES

It's ancient history unearthed

by Elizabeth Ann Biddulph

xx
Spellcraft books

Published by Spellcraft Books. Bottom Lane Farm, Leek, Staffs. England
Tel: 01538 266440

Printed by Photoprint. Leek, Staffs. England.

Published 1999

ISBN 0 9536080 0 X

Anglo-Saxon Leek

Leek *'lec'* –
Site of the holy water-spring, gift of *Erce, Goddess.*
Place of lost lows each guarded by fierce dragons.
Radiant at Solstice with two suns when time is marked by long,
stone shadows.
Enclave of Woden, ruler of wintry misty moor where demons
dark crouch in crags.
Dwelling of Ing, green God of the glade & wild wood who strikes
the soul of the waster of His kingdom with the sword of eternal
cold.

Elizabeth Ann Biddulph.

Introduction

If we are to understand how our Leek ancestors lived, it is not enough merely to note and record ancient documents, place-names and the many archaeological remains within the Staffordshire Moorlands. We need to also examine the social structures, culture, religious beliefs and the economic activities of those early 'Leek' people.

We have to try and answer the following questions; From where did our Ancestors originate? Were they in any way different from us? How did they perceive the world around them?

We need to 'explore' the local landscape and ask, 'has it always looked as it does today, or has it changed over the centuries'?- 'How has this change influenced Man's lifestyle'?

To find the answers to all these questions we must first travel back through the mists of time, almost to the dawn of Creation when Man did not yet exist.......

With grateful thanks to Trevor McGrath & the Saxon Village Project Wessex for their kindness in freely supplying the illustration for the front cover and the majority of the artwork in the Anglo Saxon/Viking chapter, all of which carry copyright *(c) 1997 Saxon Village Project Wessex BA15 1QU England . All Rights Reserved.*

All profits from this publication will go to help the vital work carried out by the Registered Medical Charity, The Arachnoiditis Trust. The Trust was founded 10 years ago to give advice and support to sufferers of Arachnoiditis and all those with long term back pain. Arachnoiditis is an increasingly common neurogenic pain syndrome found both in children and adults - thousands of people in this country suffer from it without knowing the true cause of their pain and disablement. The condition can affect every part of the body and there is no known cure. It can be caused by trauma to the spine or infections such as meningitis. However, one of the major causes during recent decades has been the widespread use of invasive back treatments - e.g. epidurals - using drugs not licensed for nor recommended for that use.. Other invasive treatments that have caused harm include myelograms, radiculograms and spinal operations, 25% of which have failed leading to neurological damage and arachnoiditis. Those who suffer from the condition often receive scant help or recognition from the Establishment. A dedicated team of medical professionals, who are themselves sufferers, is working voluntarily to bring about a change in the situation. They inform and educate the public, the medical profession and Government about all matters relating to arachnoiditis.- - with your help they could do more.

If you would like to know more about the Arachnoiditis Trust or if you feel you need help and advice, then send a stamped addressed envelope to;The Arachnoiditis Trust, P,O, Box 27, Stoneycroft, Liverpool, L13 5RS.Tel/Fax 0151 259 0222.

All measurements are written in English Feet and Inches. All weights in English Pounds and Ounces. For those who are unfamiliar with English weights/measures and coinage please refer to the following table;

12 inches = 1 foot   3 feet = 1 yard
22 yards = 1 chain   10 chains = 1 furlong
8 furlongs = 1 mile

16 ounces = 1 pound   14 pounds = 1 stone
2 stones = 1 quarter   4 quarters = 1 hundredweight
20 hundredweight = 1 ton

12 pence = 1 shilling   20 shillings = 1 pound
4 farthings = 1 penny   1 crown = 5 shillings

Periods of History

<u>Pleistocene</u> – 2,000,000 BC onwards. A time of great geological change when the land was being shaped & formed by air, fire, water & all the forces of Nature.

<u>The Ice Age</u> – Began 2 million years ago and ended 12,000 years ago.

<u>The Neolithic Age</u> - ran from 4,500BC – 2,000BC

<u>The Bronze Age.</u> – began 4,500 BC. In the area of the Peak District and the Staffordshire Moorlands metal tools and jewellery were mainly held by the upper classes . However, by 1,000 BC it was in common use in all levels of society.

<u>The Iron Age.</u> – Iron first used in the 6th century BC. This helped to improve methods of farming.

<u>The Roman Invasion</u> – The invasion began in 43 AD. The Romans entered the area of the Peak District and the Staffordshire Moorlands a generation later. They were led by the Roman General, Agricola. The Romans left in 410 AD.

<u>The AngloSaxons</u> - The AngloSaxons (the English) moved up the valley of the Trent and began to settle in the Staffordshire Moorlands in the 7th century. The Saxons were followed by <u>The Vikings.</u> By 1016 the Staffs. Moorlands were part of the Scandanavian Empire & under the 'Danelaw'. The Saxons and Vikings never left, they remained here.

<u>The Normans</u> – 1066AD invasion. Leek under Norman colonial rule by 1070AD.

<u>Medieval Period</u> – 1066 AD – 1536AD.

 ## THE BEGINNING

 280 million years ago there were no Leek Moorlands – but there was a warm, crystal-blue sea stretching as far as the horizon. Growing in parts of this shallow sea were forests of stone-lilies and coral reefs. Starfish, lampshells and molluscs grew and lived in those sunlit waters.

One of the molluscs was called an Orthoceras. It moved around under jet-propulsion and had wavy tentacles which it used to catch fish and other tiny sea creatures. Amazingly, so many shelled creatures lived and died that eventually a 2,000 feet layer of shell debris built up on the sea-bed. This layer now makes-up much of the limestone hills of the Peak District.

If you look very carefully at a piece of this local limestone you will see the various shell formations in the rock. Muddy impurities also mixed in with some of the shell remains, and this became shale.

Just a little way out in the ancient sea, new volcanoes were pouring out their burning hot larva. This larva very quickly cooled as crashing waves and swirling sea-currents surged all around it. We now call this dark volcanic rock, Toadstone because when it is wet it looks smooth and shiny like a toad's back. Toadstone was once valued by our ancestors because it was supposed to bring good luck.

Time passed and thousands of years went by. Over 200 miles away to the North, where the land met the sea, deep rushing rivers were carrying grit, minerals and sand down onto the ocean bed. The sandbanks grew longer and wider as the sea-water became fresher. When this happened a small

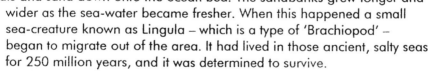 sea-creature known as Lingula – which is a type of 'Brachiopod' – began to migrate out of the area. It had lived in those ancient, salty seas for 250 million years, and it was determined to survive.

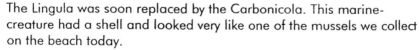 The Lingula was soon replaced by the Carbonicola. This marine-creature had a shell and looked very like one of the mussels we collect on the beach today.

As the northern rivers continued to run down into the sea, they brought with them ever more sand and grit. This gritty sediment was to become the hard Grit-stone or Millstone Grit which makes up the Roaches and the Pennine Hills that lie to the north of Leek.

The following photographs show the sandstone beds of Leek which were laid down millions of years ago when a crystal blue sea covered parts of the area. Photographs A & B were taken in Broad Street, Leek – Photo C is a close up showing the smooth water-washed pebbles that were deposited by primeval waves and rivers. Photo. D was taken in Cheddleton Road, close to Lady Dale.

A

B

Note the numerous sea/river-washed pebbles embedded in the layers of sandstone in the close-up photograph below.

C

D

The fine sand deposited around the ancient shoreline now forms the red sandstone beds which lie beneath Leek and the Churnet Valley. If you walk down Broad Street you can clearly make out, below the playground of St. Mary's R.C. School, high walls of sandstone. It's the same on the opposite side of the road. It is amazing to think that this very sandstone once formed part of the bed and shoreline of a primeaval sea.

You can find other similar sandstone beds in Mill Street, Cheddleton Road and all along the Churnet Valley. In fact, part of the town of Leek is built on sandstone, and in past centuries it was quarried and shaped into blocks for building houses. **Running below Derby Street is the actual geological line which marks the boundary between these red sandstone rocks and the grey Millstone Grit.**

Back in the distant past, time moved on. Great pressure from beneath the earth began to push the land upwards, forming wide areas of drying sandbanks interlaced with glassy streams. The strengthening winds carried in spores from the South and the East - And because the climate was pleasant and warm a jungle, made-up of

giant ferns, horse-tail weeds and trees began to take root on the newly exposed soil. The trees grew to 80 feet high. Their trunks had a diameter of 5 feet and they were covered with scales or **'Lepidodendron'.** The branches of these strange, exotic trees had soft, pointed leaves. When the ferns and trees died they formed beds of wet compost-like material. These deep layers of dead vegetation, shaped and compacted over millions of years, are the very coal-beds which now lie under the dark, heathery moors North of Leek. During the Second World War, when coal and coke was in short supply, people from Leek and the surrounding farms actually took spades and sacks to an area on the Roaches in order to dig out coal for their fires. Unfortunately, this coal was of poor quality and gave off little heat.

In the ferny, primeaval jungle there were no people, because Man had not yet evolved - but there were four legged animals which looked like newts. These creatures laid their eggs in water, and when the young hatched they had gills like fish. The baby 'newts' had to remain in the green, still-water pools between the trees until they were mature enough to live out of water.

THE ROACHES

The Roaches (Norman-French meaning 'rocks') were formed millions of years ago when the underlying beds of millstone grit were forced skyward towards the silver stars. For thousands of years they stood like gigantic, petrified waves on a slow-moving ocean. Although weathered now by centuries of ice, snow and rainwater, they still stand darkly proud against the moorland skyline. From early prehistoric times our Leek ancestors found them both fearful and awe-inspiring. Today, the Roaches and the wildlife that inhabits them are protected by the Peak District National Park Authority.

The primeaval landscape changed constantly. The sea at first swallowed up the land, then it receded. Mighty forces pushed up the numerous layers of hard rocks which crumpled and bent like soft putty. To the North, the millstone hills of the Pennines and Roaches were coming into being as part of a series of narrow, folded rocks. They looked initially like the crest of a giant wave on an angry ocean. Then the rain, wind and rivers tried to weather the hills away, but the millstone was hard and resistant, it stood its ground - The high, rocky countryside to the North of Leek bears testiment to this.

After this time, there were dramatic changes in the climate. It became dry and arrid. The forests and seas vanished as the land turned into a huge desert, complete with fiery hot winds and violent dust storms. The endless desert landscape only mellowed a little when rivers, coming down from the North in the rainy season, formed wide, shallow lakes. The geologists now call this time the Triassic Era.

The years moved swiftly by. The deserts were eventually washed away by the rivers, making the ground low and vunerable to the sea. As the salty waters returned and flooded the land, fish and ornate shelled creatures called Ammonites began to live and breed in the clean, clear water.

Sea-urchins, shelled snails and bivalves hid from predators in the rock-pools. The darting silver fish which swam together in shoals, had thick boney scales all over their bodies.
This 'armour' protected them from the large reptiles, such as 'Ichthyosaurus' which also lived in the sea. Ichthyosaurys looked very much like a crocodile and had rows of razer sharp teeth. It also had a tapering body like a whale and paddles, not fins, plus a fish-like tail. It took Nature millions of years to create the Ichthyosaurus and all the other strange creatures which lived in the ancient sea.

If Man had existed then, he would have thought his world very uninspiring - for the landscape was green and dull, with little colour. Ferny trees grew once again, but this time the reptiles or Dinosaurs living amongst the trees crawled and hopped about like kangaroos. Some of the Dinosaurs were so big and heavy, they needed to support their body by staying half submerged in deep water. The humming dragonflies and insects which flitted between the shafts of misty sunlight were preyed upon by flying reptiles with fine, silky wings. The few small mammals that existed then were extremely timid - they kept themselves safe by hiding amongst the damp rocks.

3

This Age is called the 'Jurassic Period', and for a while Leek had its very own 'JURASSIC PARK', complete with real Dinosaurs.

Some cataclysmic event was to occur at this time. One body of scientists believe a huge comet hit the earth, which caused great destruction and dramatic changes in the climate. The lumbering Dinosaurs that once walked upon that spot on the earth we now call the 'Leek' Moorlands' began to die, probably through cold or starvation.

Forests burnt and dense clouds of dark dust veiled the life-giving rays of the sun. Amazingly, many of the small shy mammals which scurried amongst the rocks survived because they were able to adapt to the changing conditions. This astronomical event may have been what ended the reign of the great reptiles on earth, and opened up the way for more intelligent mammals and Man himself to evolve. Other scientists say, the climate was deteriorating already and the impact of the comet only speeded up the inevitable end of the dinosaurs.

Whatever happened, the raging sea was to return later like some great biblical flood and cover everything that had been before.
For a while only the mountains in the far west and far north stayed above the waters, until immense forces awoke beneath the earth and started to push the bed-rock skyward.

The timeless rivers began once again their thankless task of wearing down the newly formed mountains; they softened and changed the landscape. The fertile soil deposits left by the rivers were ripe for re-generation.

Now something wonderful was about to happen. On the wings of the wind, seeds and insects were being carried in from other parts of the globe, where Mother Nature had been busy shaping and creating living things.
Woodland trees such as Birch, Apple, Alder, Oak and Beech; also poppies, buttercups, lavender, daisies, roses, thyme, hemlock and angelica were taking root and filling the grassy plains with bright colour and perfume. There were now bees, butterflies and singing birds. Across the dry land bridges, far away from the restless sea, came horses, deer, wolves and wild cats - While all around, the land was being shaped into the lovely hills and valleys we know and recognise today as, the 'Leek Moorlands'.

❄ THE COMING OF THE ICE-AGE ❄

We have now travelled millions of years through time. We have seen many geological and climatic changes in the small area of the Leek Moorlands. But there were even more changes in store in those distant times.

Across the perfect landscape the wind began to blow cold. Trees and plants started to die. The song birds and animals knew instinctively they needed to head south in search of warmer climes.

The winters brought with them the first deep snows - but when Spring came around the snowflakes did not melt. Year after year, new snow fell upon old snow. Soon the land was covered with a vast, seemingly endless snowfield. Further north across the Pennines and West across the Cheshire Plain lay thick sheets of ice - in some places it built-up to a staggering depth of 1,250 feet.

However, not all the mountains in the area were buried. The highest peaks stood out like dark demons above the pure blue ice. These peaks we call 'nunataks'. As the climate cooled even more, the solid ice began to move like water, flowing into the valleys and lowlands. In some parts of the country, the powerful ice-flows scoured out great valleys and carried huge rocks along in their wake - but the ice did not succeed in changing the basic scenery of our own district as we know it - and as the years passed this ice was again replaced by soft, sparkling-white snow fields.

The climate of the Ice Age did not remain static. There were periods when the weather was more clement. In these milder interludes the ice and snow began to melt - the summer winds blew a little warmer and the black earth showed through. Much of the ground was sodden, but in some places it was covered with low-growing arctic vegetation. There were bogs and marshes, wide shallow lakes and powerful rushing rivers, which were fed by the slowly melting snows.

From the south, herds of bison, wild horses, reindeer, sabre-tooth tigers, great woolly mammoths, woolly rhinoceros and bear moved into the area. The hardy, grazing animals were attracted by the coarse grass, lichens, dwarf shrubs and lush green moss. Some of the animals retreated south again during the winter, and they did not return if the snow-fields failed to melt during the summer.

Some of the warm periods lasted for tens of thousands of years. In fact, the weather at times became so temperate that the land was able to support Rhinoceros, Hippopotamuses, Lions and Elephants. It's amusing to think that a Hippo and his family may have wandered across the area of land that is now 'Leek'.

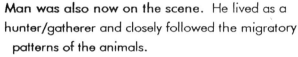

Man was also now on the scene. He lived as a hunter/gatherer and closely followed the migratory patterns of the animals.

Despite a shortage of archaeological evidence, historians know that Man has been active within our area for the last 500,000 years. Very ancient archaeological remains are easily 'lost' due to changes in landscape, natural erosion and human activity such as farming.

By this time Man knew how to make tools and weapons from stone, flint, bone and wood. He knew also how to 'create' fire, build shelters, fashion clothes from animal skins and to gather wild plants, herbs and berries for food.

Some of the tools he left behind have been discovered in this area.

<u>local finds</u>

A Prehistoric Axe Hammer was found in a wood near Leek, as well as a flint arrowhead.

A polished stone axe from this time was reported to have been found at Ashcombe, but no-one knows of its present whereabouts.

Flint arrowheads were also found in 1960, south west of Cheddleton Station.

A worked, flint knife was discovered in a cave on the Roaches. There were other finds of this nature in the earlier part of this century, but unfortunately the finders did not hand the objects into a museum. They stayed in private collections or were

THE ICE-AGE IN THE STAFFORDSHIRE MOORLANDS

For thousands of years the Staffordshire Moorlands were covered with deep snow and ice. Sabre tooth tigers stalked their prey, while woolly mammoths, bison & reindeer grazed on the tundra type grass and lichen that grew in the warmer interludes. Finally, at the end of the Ice Age, the ice and snow began to melt away – then the moorland hills echoed to the sound of thundering, roaring rivers. Great glacial lakes were formed – the above photograph taken from Morridge top looking west, shows the wide, flat area close to Bottom House/Lady Meadows where a glacial lake once existed. The drainage water from this lake carved out the well-known Combes Valley. (Combe – Old British meaning 'valley')

sold. If anyone knows of any such objects please could they give details of them to Hanley Museum.

Palaeolithic Man came here to hunt for game. He may well have built simple wooden trackways across the more difficult valley terrain to help him in his travels. At least ten caves within the Peak District have given up evidence of Palaeolithic Man's presence; these include the well known Thor's Cave, Bush Cave, Ossum's Cave and Elder Bush Cave. Some of these were being used in the late glacial times, during relatively cold conditions. This is reflected in a find of Reindeer remains from that time, which had been stored inside a stone box-like structure - an early example of a larder?!

We know that some of these hunter-gatherer people spent their summers living in caves at Creswell, Derbyshire. They did not settle in one place for long, but came only to chase and kill game such as Reindeer and Bison using spears and arrows.

They then used sharp flint tools to skin and cut up the animals they had caught. These actual tools have been found in the Creswell caves by archaeologists, and they are considered to be one of the most important finds from this age in the whole of Europe. Other finds include, quartzite tools at Harborough Rocks in Brassington, Flint in Ravenscliff Cave and a black chert hand-axe in the gravels of the River Trent.

In the later stages of the Ice-Age the climate became even warmer, and green forests replaced the white snow-fields.
The Hunter-gatherers were able to supplement their diet with nuts, plants and berries.

Whenever the winters became very cold they moved down into the lower forests. It is likely they built tree-houses to protect themselves from sodden vegetation, ground water and ferocious animals. When summer returned they moved back up onto the higher hills of the Pennines.

Animal skins and fur provided footwear and clothing. Any tools, work implements or cooking vessels they may have used would have been carved from local wood, animal bones, reindeer antlers or stone. Too much time has passed for many such items to remain intact. For this reason it was once thought that these early people were simple, less intelligent than modern man. Nothing could be further from the truth. We have thousands of years of learning and experience behind us, yet Palaeolithic Man was able to live and survive in conditions that would defeat many people now - their lives and hunting expeditions would, by neccesity, have been well planned and organised. It is a fact that the vast majority of people living today would be totally incapable of gathering or hunting-down their own food in the wild - and a great many would not have the faintest idea how to build a shelter or even light a fire without the use of modern equipment.

The advance and retreat of the snowfields and ice was continue for another two million years. - It was during one of these retreats that there came about a change in sea-level around the coast of Britain due to the melting of the heavy ice-caps. Our small island home became separated from the rest of Europe. This meant that both the animals and hunters living here could no longer 'migrate' east. When the ice returned, again, they were able to reach the mainland of Europe by walking across the frozen Channel.

With the Ice-Age finally over, deciduous trees and forests returned en-mass. The first to take root were the seeds of the graceful Silver Birch tree, then the Alder and the mighty Oak. However, as the average temperature soared above 10 degrees C and the annual rainfall exceeded 5 inches, these areas of light woodland were soon over-run by pine trees invading from the south.

For some time the Leek Moorlands, along with the rest of England, resembled a great pine forest. Inside the forest it was dark and errie. The soil was peaty, and during the autumn months toadstools would appear. But these forests did give shelter to some animals during the winter and they provided shade in summer. Resin sucking insects buzzed and caterpillars crawled amongst the sharp needles on the branches. There were birds too, such as finches which lived on hard seeds and forest berries. There was very little for the larger animals - they grazed on the few hillsides where the silver birch trees still hung on.

8

As the climate warmed up even more, the pine forests died away, and they were replaced by deciduous trees. The Leek Moorlands now had high forests of Oak, Elm, Ash and many other species running down from the hills into the valleys. Flowering bulbs and a profusion of seed bearing flowers grew both in the woods and outside.

FIRE IN THE FOREST

As the world changed around him, so Man also had to change. Britain was once again an island, and it became even more essential for men to utilise all the local natural resources. Now was the time when those hunter/gatherers first started to clear the trees using fire. This was not done in order to grow crops, but to attract grazing animals in spring, when the first lush, green shoots of grass showed above the dark ground. Man soon discovered that it was easier to bring the animals to a place which suited him, rather than use precious energy chasing after them.

This important development led on eventually to the settled practice of 'penning-in' and farming of animals, as well as the controlled growing of choice herbs, fruit and crops.

THE MAGIC OF TREES

Early man also started to avoid the lower lying forests. These spelt danger and darkness, and it was likely in those early times that people first became aware of the wonder, the 'magic' of trees. Perhaps here was the beginning of his belief in tree spirits. He would note the difference between the slender 'female' Silver Birch and the soaring, dark 'demon' pine tree, the mighty strength of the 'male' oak and the 'benevolence' of the hazel and wild apple which freely gave him nuts and fruit.

THE HUNT

Men still left their now more permanent camps to hunt for animals, while the women and children did the gathering. The male parties set-up 'hunting' camps on the highest ground above the river valleys. This gave them a view of the surrounding countryside, and they were able to plot the movements of game. Historians believe Man was now using tame 'companion' wolves to help him in the hunt and for the protection of the 'home' camp. The higher wooded hillsides held not only wild boar and red deer, but also wild bees with their rich supplies of honey. This natural sweetener would have been considered a precious and valuable addition to the daily diet. Wild apple and pear trees provided fruit during the autumn months, along with elderberry, blackberry and the bright red berries of the mountain ash.

THE FIRST FARMERS OF LEEK

Archaeologists know that people were farming in the gritstone areas of the Peak District as early as 4,5000 BC. In fact, the Peak was one of the most important agricultural regions in the country at that time because the soil was light, rich and easy to work. We also know that a thriving farming community was in existence within the geographical area of Leek during the Neolithic/Bronze/Iron Age period.

Religion was central to the daily life of those early Leek farmers – **And they actually built a magnificent burial mound or 'low'** close to the site of the present day Westwood Road recreation ground. It carried the name '*Cock Low*' or '*Catteslowe -*'. The name derives from the **Anglo Saxon** word '*catt*' meaning '*wild cat*'. and is also related to the **Old Norse (Viking)** '*kati*', again meaning '*cat*'. In the 18th century it was referred to as the, '*Great Low*'. This famous low gave rise to Leek's ancient title of, '*Leek & Low*'.

Excavations and surveys by archaeologists both within the Peak District and other areas of the country show that, such burial mounds were '**non-random**', in that they were always sited either at the edge of, or in the centre of, the land (field system) which was being farmed – or on higher 'topographical sites' designed to 'overlook' the field system and the community which raised them. In fact, every community or settlement had its own barrows or burial mounds.

So, just what purpose did burial mounds serve?
Because ownership of good farming land meant a plentiful supply of food with its subsequent wealth, leading to power, these mounds were built to mark out boundaries on territory. For this very reason all mounds, including the one sited close to Westwood Road, would have contained the bodies and grave goods of the original founders and later members of the community and their families. Those who were not given the honour of being buried in the mound would have shared open ground cemeteries.

In Leek, as in many other such burial places, the site would originally have been an open ritual area marked out by a stone boundary. The huge mound itself would not have been built until after a number of ground burials had already taken place there.
The Leek mound would have fulfilled an important symbolic, religious role in regard to fertility of the land and the success of the crops. It would have also acted as a warning for any others wishing to trespass on the territory. It told everyone

THE MOVE INTO FARMING.

The countryside we see around Leek today is the result of hundreds of centuries of slow, gradual change. As the early, prehistoric people of the Staffordshire Moorlands moved from hunting into farming, they too left their mark. What we observe now is a record of that ancient culture. Much of the rich birch-oak tree cover was removed during the Bronze and Iron Age periods, and the land given over to self-sufficient farming.

Throughout the years small, prehistoric sites laid down a settlement pattern that has been built upon by later generations.

The very early Leek farmers were basically herdsmen who bred and grazed their stock on grassland between areas of woodland. Having established small farming settlements they enjoyed a strict economic, religious and social order. As the decades passed, well cultivated fields took the place of trees.

By the time of the Roman Conquest the 'Lands of Leek' had been farmed for many centuries. It was what is now termed, *'old country'* made up of farming clans who shared a common culture.

Westwood Road Recreation Ground – In past times it was the likely site of a Bronze/IronAge field system connected to the farming clan who constructed the 'CockLow' burial mound.

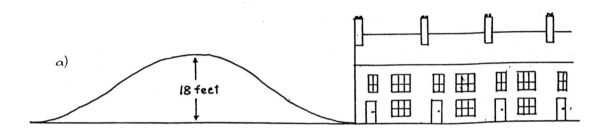

THE 'COCKLOW' or 'CATTES LOWE' BURIAL MOUND – (very ancient place name derived from Anglo Saxon word 'catt' meaning 'wild cat' & Old Norse-Viking 'kati' also meaning 'cat')

a)

18 feet

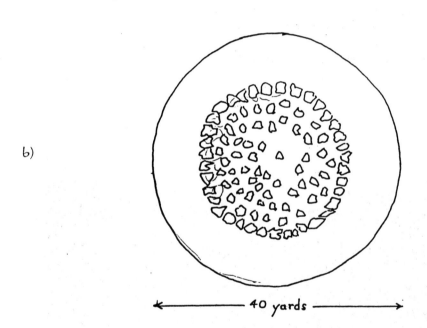

b)

←——— 40 yards ———→

a) The BronzeAge Burial mound was over 18ft. high (Note how it compares in height to a modern town house). It was 40 yards in diameter.

b) The plan illustrates the possible lay-out of the low at ground level.

who passed that way that the farming clan living there had definite rights to the land. They had in other words, 'staked out their claim' – And because religion, with its ritual burials, was such a powerful guiding force in those far off times, it may well have been that the spirits of dead ancestors, especially to outsiders, were something to be feared – for they watched over and protected the land.

We now need to ask the following questions, *'What happened to the Leek burial mound'? 'How was it built'? 'What did it contain'?*

WHAT HAPPENED TO LEEK'S MAGNIFICENT BURIAL MOUND?

To answer this question we need to go back to the year 1907, when Leek's most noted ancient burial mound was destroyed by an insensitive and exceedingly short-sighted town council.

Standing between Waterloo Road, Messr's Broster's Mill and Spring Gardens, on part of the property owned by a Mrs. Watt, was an 18ft. high Neolithic/Bronze Age burial mound. It was described at the time as**, 'magnificent'**. It was known locally as *'Cock Low' or 'Catteslow'*.. And it was reported that a second, similar low or burial mound had also stood in the vicinity, but had apparently been destroyed earlier by those who had built Messers. Wardle & Davenport's Mill. (*Unfortunately there appears to be no documented archaeological record of this second low*).

However, we do know that it came to the ears of the Rev. W. Berresford that 'Cock Low' / 'Catteslow' was to be destroyed in order to make way for the town's development. The Rev. was greatly alarmed, and fully understanding that such an act would amount to vandalism, went at once to Sir Thomas Wardle and Mr. W.S. Brough to enlist their help. The Rev. Beresford was a man ahead of his time, and fully understood the historical and religious value of such a site. He appealed to the Town Council and asked them to spare the mound. Tragically he failed, and the following are the actual words of the Rev. W. Berrisford who proclaimed himself to be 'greatly averse to the opening of such a sacred thing'.

"I watched its demolition with great regret. It was a mighty mound and as you stood on the curb of the new street, the highest storey only of the four-storey mill adjacent was visible over its top.

The first of many loads taken from it revealed its construction to be layers of strange white sand, alternating with black charcoal sand.....Some interesting discoveries were made.

Near the top of the mound, on the south side, a fine urn with a double lip for carrying it tumbled out that September day, falling to pieces, but displaying its contents. These were first of all, strange to say, **a little heart neatly carved in stone** and then a small parcel of hacked and chopped up bones – both animal bones **and bits of a child's skull**..... Lower down, pockets of charcoal were found and on the ground level was **a mass of stones not quite a circle,** dyed red with the washing down of rains through the red sandstone above them.... a further yield *[of finds]* was then made. A drain was driven along the foot of the mound and in the sand which had filled it were traces of **brilliant blue** which Sir Thomas Wardle kindly examined and pronounced to be **woad** – the material used by the earliest Britons for tattooing their faces. The finding of the urn on the top of the mound not far from the iron ring *(jewellery?)* shows that only the more recent human remains therein buried has been preserved.......The carved stone heart which fell out of the mound with the urn and bones was almost a **unique specimen of such like** ancient work'.

It is difficult for anyone who cares about their heritage to read this report without feeling disturbed and angry. It should make the people of Leek feel extremely sad that such a magnificent historical site, with all its valuable archaeological data and unique finds, was so easily lost. **– And how terrible to think that a little child's grave was desecrated so wantonly!**

If the mound still stood today, it would provide a special and unique attraction for visitors to the town. What made matters worse was the fact that in 1907, when some of the Town Councillors received the appeal to save the mound, they tried to pretend the mound was not old and that they could even remember it being constructed! This was to make certain the development work went ahead.

This 'blind-eye' attitude by the old Council seems very familiar. How many councillors today still fall for the pseudo-babble of greedy modern-day developers who hold up the false promise of making Leek a rich town, in return for the demolition or spoiling of the town's heritage and the violation of its beautiful green fields and woodlands? How many ancient sites and how much historical/archaeological evidence has been lost in Leek by road widening, the pulling down/alteration/damage of old buildings and shop-fronts, the unnecessary out-of-character modern housing and industrial development? **The answer is, 'A great deal'!**

You only have to look around you to see just how scarred Leek's green landscape has become, all the way from Mount Road in the north to the River Churnet in the south. Modern box houses have been allowed to almost spill over into Leek's only green park. Many visitors and even television/newspaper reporters come to St. Edward's Church Yard (*one of Leek's most ancient and holiest sites*) at Midsummer to watch the famous double sunset. What do they see as they gaze down onto the once beautiful valley below? You only have to visit the Westwood/Wall-Bridge Estates or near-by Cheddleton to appreciate how badly thought out housing policy has completely ruined the once beautiful rolling hills and dales!

Tourism is now one of the most profitable, fastest growing industries in the country. But tourists won't be attracted to Leek if it becomes nothing more than a carbon-copy of sprawling, grubby Hanley/Stoke and other soulless towns with their identical shopping centres, endless housing estates, dirty bus-stations, industrial sites and cloned supermarkets. Just two hundred years ago Burslem and Stoke-on-Trent were considered two of the prettiest villages in Staffordshire; they were surrounded by emerald fields, hills and dales; the air was pure, the rivers crystal clear. They held a wealth of valuable historical and archaeological sites. Then the black weed of industrialisation and development spread its roots everywhere -We can see the devastating results today. It should serve as a dire warning to all. If Leek wishes to become a well-known, attractive tourist centre, then all the modern-day developers need first to be 'run out of town'!

With that said, we can return to our ancient burial mound.

The Leek mound had been partly excavated by schoolmaster, Samual Carrington from Wetton, sixty years earlier in 1847. Carrington was the helper of the famous Thomas Bateman, Secretary of the newly founded British Archaeological Association. The following is a section from the actual report of that dig.

'On the 29th of December we proceeded to excavate 'Cock Low Barrow' close to the town of Leek; a large mound forty yards diameter and eighteen feet high composed of sand and raised above the natural surface of red sand, unmixed with any other tint. After cutting a square six yards each way down the centre to the depth of five feet, we came on a layer of ashes and charcoal resting on a stratum of white sand. Among the former were some small pieces of urn, a few calcined human bones and a round-edged instrument of flint. Beside this we observed nothing.'

A report of this excavation appeared later in the, 'Derby Mercury'.

Ground plan of stone circles &
Tumuli found on Eyam Moor
(Bateman)

It is obvious from this report and the newspaper article that archaeology was in its infancy. Archaeologists had not yet learnt the precise techniques of careful, respectful excavation. Carrington had completely missed the later, most valuable finds – for it was noted at that time that, 'this mound provided nothing for Mr. Bateman's own private museum'. Although the mound was forty yards in diameter, Carrington only excavated down in a square six yards by six yards.

HOW 'COCK LOW' / 'CATTESLOW' WAS CONSTRUCTED

Looking at the eye-witness account by the Rev. Berrisford and working from the base of the mound upwards, we can see first of all that at ground level there was a 'mass of stones, not quite a circle'. There was no mention of stones in Carrington's report. If we take the report literally, then the word 'mass' would mean, 'a dense collection' of stones. So, we can't be certain of the size or shape of each individual stone, if they were piled together like a collapsed structure or if they were laid out in a circular pattern. We can only say (*based on many other similar excavated Neolithic/Bronze Age lows*) that either, the stones could have been the remains of a collapsed burial chamber over which the later mound and subsequent burials had been placed, or more likely, they were a round circle of stones originally placed there to mark out a religious ritual area. The great burial mound had then been built up over a long period of time.

The report does not state what type of stone it was, only that it had been, 'dyed red with the washing down of rains through the red sandstone above'. This suggests that the 'base' stones were not made of sandstone, but some other type of rock. If this is so then, the stones must have been transported into the area from outside, perhaps the northern millstone grit region, as sandstone is the natural underlying rock in the Westwood area.

This leads on to the fact that mounds of this type were usually built over a long period of time, using locally gathered earth, plants and turf – All of which were collected when the ground was being cleared for the growing of crops. The early Leek farmers would naturally have been very practical people. As soil is heavy, especially when wet, and as everything had to be moved physically by hand, they would not have wanted to carry the ground spoil very far.

At the time the high, dark red mound would have stood out starkly above the

14

surrounding green landscape.

We now have to surmise what might have been, as we are not working from documented evidence. So, let's assume that the second mound on the site of Wardle & Davenport's mill referred to in 1907 was, more or less, of similar design and make-up, and may well have marked out the outer boundary of the Bronze Age field system. It is possible there were many other such burial mounds/lows in the vicinity, but they would have been destroyed by weathering, ploughing and urbanisation in the long centuries leading up to the 1900's, and thus remain unrecorded.

It was stated that the 'Cock Low' / 'Catteslow' mound was eighteen feet high. We can assume that the mound was originally somewhat higher, as allowance needs to be made for the thousands of years of weathering and erosion. It was 40 yards or 120 feet in diameter.

As to the discovery of the brilliant, light blue substance (*woad)* in the early 20th century drain at the foot of the mound – Woad is now considered to be a native plant (*Isatis tinctoria*) . It was introduced into this country during Prehistoric times for use in religious ritual decoration and later for the dyeing of cloth. It grows mainly in chalk or clay areas. We have no way of knowing if those who built 'Cock Low' / 'Catteslow' gathered the woad locally, or if they acquired it through trading with clans in other areas of the country. We also can't be certain just how deep the 1907 drain was dug. So, how did this woad actually get into the spoil from the mound clearance?

There are three possibilities. If the 1907 drain was say, two feet down or more, then this could suggest that there were underground burials within the mound area, and that the blue woad had been used to decorate the dead bodies or grave goods. It does not suggest cremation of bodies. The woad had then leached into the surrounding soil. The workmen were not reported at that time to have dug below the natural ground level in the middle of the 'circle' itself., so they would have missed any remains/finds which may have been buried there.

If the blue woad did not come from an earlier 'underground' burial, then it may have been washed down from non-cremated burials or from grave-goods (even cloth) within the mound itself. Also much evidence would have been missed or destroyed at the time. The third possibility is that it could have remained from the time when the area with the 'ring of stone' was being used for religious ritual purposes.

15

It is worth mentioning here that in 1859, workmen who were carrying out drainage work in **Birchall Meadows** in Leek , 'broke ground on a very slightly elevated barrow and found therein a cairn of stones and a cinery urn ornamented with the herring-bone pattern and containing a soft moist matter (Stafford Papers).

From this description we can say that, this provides evidence of another Neolithic/Bronze or Iron Age burial/ritual site. This cinery urn appears very similar to the one found in 'Cock Low' and the 'soft moist matter' may well have been burnt human remains/ashes.

The Rev. Berrisford in 1907 reported – 'layers of strange white sand alternating with black charcoal sand', in 'Cock Low'. This suggests that cremation took place there. Both cremation and normal burial of bodies were used during the Neolithic/Bronze Age period. In around 1,000 BC new settlers moved into the area of the Peak District and they introduced a special ritual of cremation for the dead. Ashes were sometimes placed inside an urn, which for some reason was then buried upside down. Because of this these people became known as, 'The Urn People'.

The coming of these new settlers marked a change in religious custom. Before their arrival some of the dead had been buried in stone chambered tombs or cists, like the one found at **Birchall Meadows,** but these man-made structures fell out of use and the dead began to be buried under mounds of earth. However, these stone tombs were not always abandoned; new earth mounds were merely constructed over the top.

Not every urn was used for cremation, and many contained offerings of drink or food. An urn with a double lip was discovered in the 'Cock Low' mound, along with the carved stone heart. Simple grave goods like this were common; sometimes there could be coloured beads, round buttons, bronze daggers or necklaces. It was once thought that the quality of the grave goods reflected only the wealth of the deceased person in the community. This is now known to be inaccurate. In fact grave goods were used as a symbol of the role the person played while still alive. Bronze Age Chieftains were buried with their armour, weapons and rich metal ornaments, such as armlets and torcs, because these objects represented their position as ruler of the clan. Those buried with axes and daggers would have been the warriors and protectors of the community. Women were buried with beads and flint work tools. We can only imagine what the carved stone heart found with the child's remains in the 'Cock Low' mound represented, but similar objects today denote affection and love.

The finding of 'an iron ring' at the site is also mentioned. Although not described in detail, it could well have been a torc or arm bracelet. If in fact it was made of iron, as stated in the Rev. Berrisford's report, then it would have been a relic from the Iron Age.

Carrington, in 1847, only brought out some small pieces of broken urn, a few pieces of calcined human bone and a round-edged instrument of flint. His description of the urn tells us little, however the calcined bone again suggests cremation. The flint instrument could have been the remains of a tool or weapon. He also described a layer of ashes, charcoal and white sand. All of which supports the theory of religious cremation of the dead on the site.

Summing up the evidence of the 'Cock Low' mound it would appear that the site contained a number of burials, and may well have been used over many generations. It was most certainly a religious ritual site for the local community at that time.

OTHER ARCHAEOLOGICAL FINDS IN THE
STAFFORDSHIRE MOORLANDS

Around this time, the population of the country as a whole was increasing, and this is shown in the great number of burial mounds/lows and archaeological finds discovered in the Staffordshire Moorlands.

Two Bronze Age vessels/urns were found just outside Leek, at Upper Hulme, in 1883. The actual discovery site was on the outer rim of the Goldsitch Valley, north of Hen Cloud. Unfortunately, only one of the two vessels was presented to the Leek Museum.

This particular vessel is 3-4 inches wide at the mouth, 2.9 inches at the base and 5.7 inches high. It is made up from a hard, brown gritty fabric and is decorated in two parts. On one collar there is what is called an 'incised double chevron design'. Below the shoulder of the vessel are incised horizontal and vertical lines. It is a type of vessel that would have been used by the 'Urn People'. The actual design of the urn is rare. It contained charred bones and flint, which suggests it is a burial urn used for religious cremation. The second vessel found was a wine or water bottle, and evidence at the time suggested that it had been buried alongside a whole, unburnt body. Both vessels were slate colour.

Urn found at Winhill (Bateman)

Examples of local archaeolgical Bronze Age finds in the Staffordshire Moorlands

a) Early black & white photograph of
    the Urn with a double lip found in
    Cocklow burial mound in Leek
    It was placed there by the
    Neolithic/BronzeAge Leek Farmers.

b) Early photograph of the neatly
    Carved stone heart found inside
    The Cocklow Bronze Age Urn

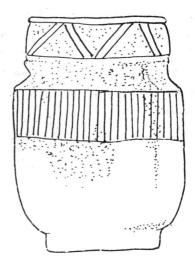

c) A drawing of one of the two Bronze
    Age urns found at Upper Hulme.
    This pottery belonged to the
    'Urn People' of Leek.

The placing of grave goods, such as weapons and drinking vessels, in burial mounds does seem to indicate that the people of those early times believed in an after-life.

On Morridge, nr. Leek, a burial mound was opened in 1850, but no finds were made. Such sites may well have been 'robbed' in past times by those who had no respect for the dead they contained.

At Blackbrook Farm, Ipstones, a stone built cist with a paved floor was found by workmen - (a cist is a burial placed carved out from, or constructed from, stone). Again no actual objects were found.

At Sharpcliffe Estate, Ipstones, both a burial cist and pottery were discovered by workmen digging for gravel. Unfortunately, the finds were destroyed at that time. Quite a number of burial mounds survive in the Ipstones area with names such as 'Blakelow'. This is an Anglo-Saxon word and means 'a bleak or dark low'.

At 'Mare Hill', three burials were excavated containing flint spears and a round-headed bronze dagger; obviously the burial place of a Bronze Age warrior farmer.

There is a Bronze Age mound at 'Stanlow', Longsdon nr. Leek.

A flat decorated bronze axe (Bronze Age) was found at Endon.

A Bronze Age sword was discovered at Alton. The sword is now in Hanley Museum.

Items made from Irish gold consisting of a gold chain and bells, a gold torc and a golden bracelet were discovered at Stanton, as well as Iron Age coins. One of these coins was a Centra or Gaulish type. Both can be seen at the Ashmolean Museum in Oxford.

At Wetton, a globular pot from this period of history was found.

'Lamber Low' in Waterhouses has a cist which measures 3 feet by 2 feet internally.

Bronze Age dagger
(minus handle) found by
Bateman in 'Dow Low'.

Stone Burial Cist found at 'Longlow'
Wetton (Bateman) Similar to those
Found at Morridge , Ipstones & Birchall- Leek.

Another cist was found at 'Mouse Low' in Grindon. This was constructed with three sides, using three large stones. The forth side was open. The bottom or floor was paved with blue limestone.

The 'Bridestones' nr Congleton is a very well known and outstanding burial site. There, a large paved stone passage way, made up of large slabs of stone, was laid leading to a stone burial chamber. After the chamber had been constructed it was covered with earth. There are many more burial places similar to this within the Peak District.

'Falcon Low Cave' at Waterhouses, is a burial site from this time. Six people were found buried there, two adults and four children. Inside the low the archaeologists also found flints, the bones of a dog, wild cat, pig, sheep and water vole skeletons which are very common in local barrows. Also discovered there were the bones of an Arctic Hare. This type of hare does not exist in the area today. It does not necessarily mean that the climate was colder during that time, it is just that many wild creatures have been driven out by the activities of modern man. The entrance to the 'Falcon Low' cave had been blocked with stones. It is a very steep, exhausting climb up to this low, and it was obviously positioned there to overlook the surrounding countryside.

Leek Archaeology Society carried out some excavation work here and finds included ancient animal remains.

The 'Nine Ladies' stone circle on Stanton Moor. (Bateman)

The famous 'Thor's Cave' in the Manifold Valley has also given us interesting remains from this time. The following is an extract from a report on an excavation there carried out by Thomas Bateman;

'On the 9th. of September, we opened a mound nine yards across nr. Thor's Cave. We turned most of it over, finding it to consist of red earth mixed with chert....charcoal, bits of bone, burnt and unburnt, and pieces of stag's horn. Near the centre, about a foot below the surface we found two very curious vessels; one of rather globular form, four inches high, carved in sand-stone like the Irish Urns, and ornamented by four grooves round the outside. About a foot from it was another equally curious vessel, which may be styled a bronze pan or kettle, four inches high and six inches in diameter, with a slender iron bow like a bucket handle. It had been first cast, then hammered, and very slightly marked with horizontal ridges. The stone vessel was found in upright position and the bronze one was inverted. Above it were traces of decayed wood. Stone vessels of this kind are rarely found in England, but they are common in the north of Scotland and the Shetland Isles.' – 'Diggings p.172'

Bateman carried out hundreds of excavations on burial mounds in Staffordshire, the Staffordshire Moorlands and Derbyshire, and he made detailed reports of his many finds. Another of these excavations took place at 'Farlow' or 'Druid's Barrow', Cauldon, Waterhouses, nr. Leek.

'Druid's Barrows' ♓
'On the 21st. April, 1849 another barrow in the same neighbourhood called 'Farlow' was opened. It is twenty-one yards in diameter, consisting of a level area surrounded by an elevated border known as the 'Druid's Barrow'. Digging to the depth of four feet in the centre, through earth and stones, we discovered the skeleton of a young person laid upon the ribs of an ox or other large animal placed transversely to the human at regular intervals side by side. At the north end of the barrow was a rock grave the bottom of which was about two feet beneath the turf, containing the skeleton of another young person accompanied by a very neatly-ornamented vase, five inches high, and nine instruments of white flint, eight of which lay together in the corner of the grave, whilst the ninth was found in the middle. The vase retained an upright position, having been placed upon a flat stone, and likewise protected by another standing on edge by its side. On the south and east sides of the mound were remains of two other bodies, neither of which yielded any article worth of notice.' – Diggings p. 132/3.

Extracts from Bateman's Reports on Excavations on Burial Lows in the Staffordshire Moorlands

Batman excavated a great many Burial Lows within the Staffordshire Moorlands. Below is just a small selection from his reports.

Report 1. Elaborately ornamented Bronze Age Drinking Cup found with skeleton in Barrow nr. Castern, Staffs.

"On the 29th July, 1846 a large tumulus (burial low) was examined at Castern, nr. Wetton, Staffs...that part of the mound (the centre) being constructed of loose stones which were found to continue below the natural surface, to the depth of 4 feet, making an entire depth of 8 feet from the summit. At this depth lay the original and most important interment, in a square cist cut out of the rock. The skeleton lay on its left side......accompanied by the most elegant and elaborately ornamented drinking cup or vase. (it) was placed in an upright position ..and exhibited signs of being two thirds full (of liquid) at the time of burial. At a short distance from the centre of the barrow were the remains of a fire which had been made upon a flat stone.

Another body was found ..within 6 inches of the summit; it owed its preservation mainly to a large flat stone which had been laid over it. "

Report 2 – Alstonfield, Staffs.

Ornamented Vase with incised lines, lip thickened and two edges lower down tapering at the base.
Five & half inches high. Found beneath a large stone in a barrow on 'Narrowdale Hill', Alstonfield, Staffordshire, Sept. 1846.

Report 3 – Decorated Vase found with Skeleton of a Child, Mare Hill, Staffs.

"....We continued the excavation at right angles...at the depth of about 2 feet from the surface, was the skeleton of a child... accompanied by a neatly-ornamented vase, 5 inches high, which was placed by the side of a flat stone set on its edge for its protection. Half a yard further on ...were a good arrowhead of flint and a perforated bone pin having been placed within a small inverted urn, Near the same place a piece of fused lead and (another child)..."

(NB. The inverted urn would suggest this was a burial of the 'Urn People)

Report 4 – Drinking Cup found with skeleton, Mouse Low, Deepdale, Staffordshire. "On June 21ˢᵗ.

'1848 opened a barrow between Deepdale and the village of Grindon, called 'Mouse Low'. ...In the centre was a cist constructed of three large, flat stones, the fourth side being open. It was paved with very thin slabs of blue limestone, and contained the skeleton of a very large and strongly built man.....near whose head was a peculiarly elegant and well finished drinking cup, 8 ½ inches high inside of which were two implements cut from the ribs of a large animal, a spear head and two beautiful barbed arrows of white flint. Outside the cup were two more arrows. ...As far as our trench extended (5 yards) it exposed a row of large boulders of hard red grit(stone) laid out on the surface of the natural soil".

(N.B The reference to the large boulders would suggest that these were originally placed there to mark out a religious ritual area)

Report 5 – Elaborately decorated Drinking Cup found at 'Green Low' with skeleton, (made of) red clay with various patterns formed of dotted lines 7 ½ inches high found with skeleton on Alsop Moor, April 1844.

Report 6 – Vase of Globular form found with Skeleton in "Wetton Hill Barrow' Staffordshire, May, 1849.

(A second cutting was made into the barrow following a previous one carried out earlier)

"Mr Carrington ….made a cutting from the opposite side…which showed that in some places the materials were large stones..After removing the stones to a depth of 1 yard we found a skeleton accompanied by one..flint arrow. The skull was remarkably short and elevated like the Turkish skull…
we found another skeleton deposited ..in the cist (which) was roughly made of large limestones..before the face was a very beautiful vase 4 ½ inches high with a fluted border and four perforated 'ears'.

Report 7 – Sepulchral Urn found in barrow (low) on Narrowdale Hill, nr. Alstonefield, Staffordshire, Sept. 1846.

"..opened a small barrow on the summit of Narrow-dale Hill..in the centre, inverted over a deposit of burnt bones, was a large un-ornamented urn which was rested upon a large stone, level with the rock; a flint ..was deposited along with the bones beneath the urn. The large stone, being removed, was found to be the cover of a cist cut down in the rock and filled with soil. ..at one corner of this vault stood a neatly-ornamented urn in perfect condition. On the Alstonefield side was found a neat little cist made of four flat limestones. ..Amongst the heap of (burnt) bones were a neat arrowhead of flint, a bone button or ornament perforated with three holes for attachment to the dress and a piece of Stags Horn….

Early photograph of the 'very beautiful 6 ½ in Drinking cup found with 2 other elegant cups & skeleton of young person + 2 children found in Barrow of Stanshope, Staffs. Nov. 1849

THE WORD 'LOW' IN PLACE-NAMES

It is often possible to locate Neolithic/Bronze/Iron Age and later Roman and Anglo-Saxon burial sites from place-names. The word *'low'* usually points to the site of an ancient burial mound.

'Low Hill' on the Ashbourne Road leading out of Leek is one possible example, along with all the other ones mentioned previously. There is also *'Cauldon Low'*, the present site of an unsightly limestone quarry. We do not know for certain the exact site of the burial place at Low Hill - this requires further field investigations. However we do know that a number of lows at *Cauldon Low* were totally destroyed by the quarrying. This is a great pity. It would not have been beyond the realms of possibility for the quarry owners to have preserved these extremely historically valuable lows and the unique and beautiful limestone caves called, *'The Fairy Caves'* which existed there.

The Midwinter sun once rose behind Cauldon Low, now all that is left is a terrible, ugly scar on the landscape that grows bigger by the year.

THE GREEN DRAGON

Following on from this we can explore a very interesting concept. We know that the early Christian churches were often deliberately built on much earlier pagan, pre-Christian religious sites. Therefore the question needs to be asked, "Is St. Edward's Church in Leek built on just such a sacred site?"

Neolithic/Bronze/Iron Age monuments were special places where religious rites and ceremonies were carried out. It is believed, by historians, that these actual monuments were used to celebrate the passing of the seasons, the changing of the fertility of the land and, more significantly in the case of the site of St. Edward's Church, *'the astronomical events which marked out the yearly cycle'*.

It is agreed by archaeologists that, there is strong evidence to suggest that these religious sites were aligned to be important at certain times of the year, such as the winter and summer solstice or where the sun or moon rose or set behind a prominent feature in the landscape.

☼ ☼ Consider then the famous double sunset which takes place behind Bosley cloud every Midsummer and which can only be observed from the churchyard of St. Edward's Church.

Add to this the important fact that these ritual sites were often deliberately placed where there were distinctive water-springs – and we also know such springs often became places for both pagan and Christian religious ceremony.

We know Leek and much of its Moorlands had many Neolithic/Bronze/Iron Age farming communities. Surely these early people, so closely tied to the land and the seasons for their very survival, could not have failed to observe the amazing astronomical Midsummer spectacle which still takes place every year at. St. Edward's churchyard! Would that not have been the very place for our ancient Leek ancestors to celebrate the passing of the seasons, to carry out religious rituals and raise a sacred low for the burial of their dead?

It is a documented fact that the sites of these ancient lows continued to be used, added to and recognised throughout the following Roman period and into the later pagan/Christian Anglo Saxon era. The Anglo Saxons being highly superstitious and wishing only to protect all their ancestors' burial sites made great play, both in their legends, poetry and literature, of the fact that,

'lows are places where fierce dragons do dwell'
and were therefore places to be both feared and respected.

In the 1500's or maybe in the 1400's, a building was raised, in the town of Leek, which is now the present day site of the 'Swan' public house. It is recorded that the earliest name for that building was, The Green Dragon'. In the 1600's the open fields which extended down the present West Street area and which were over-looked by St. Edward's Church were known as, The Dragon's Crofts'. Could these old names be a throw-back, a folk-memory from the distant past when a large, Bronze Age burial mound stood silhouetted against the fiery, midsummer sky just across the way?

'FAWFIELD HEAD' BURIAL LOW.

The round barrow or burial 'low' is the most prevalent and wide spread monument of the Bronze Age in the Staffordshire Moorlands. These lows were always sited at the edge, in the centre of or over looking the land being farmed. The photograph below shows 'Fawfield Head' burial low' (AngloSaxon name meaning 'far field'). Fawfield Head Low stands clear against the skyline and almost conceals the stone & tiled barn which is built alongside.

The 'Cocklow' burial mound, constructed by the Bronze Age farmers of Leek, was a huge, monumental low by comparison. It is more than likely that other such lows once existed within the geographical area of Leek, for example at the present site of St. Edward's Church. Chieftains /Princes and those in the upper classes of the farming clan were buried in such lows.

THE ROUND HOUSES OF LEEK

Elizabeth Ann Biddulph

The Bronze and Iron Age farmers of Leek lived in small villages made up of large impressive round houses very like the one illustrated above. The walls were fashioned from wattle and daub and these supported an extensive, expertly thatched roof. Note the ornately carved wooden doorframe and the hole, set at the apex of the roof, which allowed smoke to escape from the internal, central hearth. Some of the houses are likely to have had the cremated remains of a respected family ancestor buried under the floor. This would have been marked with a carved wooden shrine.

Each house held an extended family group. Outside was a fenced area for growing herbs and vegetables - Beyond this lay cultivated fields and the many burial lows which acted as boundary markers and symbols of ownership.

Round house villages would have been connected with burial lows such as 'Catteslow' or 'Cocklow', also the ancient low which once stood on the present site of St. Edward's Church, 'Birchall', 'Low Hill', plus numerous other sites within the Staffordshire Moorlands.

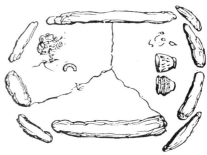

Ground plan of cist at Arbor Low (Bateman)

SOME OTHER LOCAL ANCIENT MONUMENTS

There are other religious monuments from this time close to the Staffordshire Moorlands. One of these is Arbor Low Stone Circle which stands south of Monyash. It is actually one of the largest late Neolithic stone circles in the whole of England, and would have been a very important religious site in those early times.

Forty large slabs of limestone lie on the ground pointing towards the centre of the circle. In the middle of these are several larger stones. The two entrances to this ancient circle are set on the compass bearings of N.N.E. and S.S.W. Arbor Low stands at a height of 1,200 feet and can be seen from many vantage points in the surrounding landscapes.

It is known that the original place for religious ceremonies was not inside the Arbor Low henge itself, but on an adjacent mound called, 'Gib Hill'. This is a long barrow upon which is set a round, Bronze Age barrow - one of two built at that time long ago. A stone cist was discovered there, and below that were cremated human remains.

Evidence of hand-made pottery was found at the site. This pottery is believed to have originated from the geographical area around Peterborough. Archaeologists now believe that the stone circle was used on important occasions relating to the four seasons and the position of the planets and stars in the heavens.

We can safely assume that the clans living within the Leek Moorlands would have known about and visited Arbor Low using an ancient Prehistoric trackway which ran through Leek. As well as stone monuments, people from that time were also raising wooden monuments. From recent excavations in other parts of the country it is believed that the uprights for these monuments were intricately carved. They would have very much resembled standing stones, but would have been easier to construct. It is thought that these monuments were topped with lintels and thatching. They would have been used as meeting places and ceremonial centres. The theory has been recently put forward by historians that, the builders of Stone Henge may well have based their 'blue-print' for the famous henge on similar, wooden monuments.

Arbor Low is regarded as special because it would have needed very large-scale organisation and co-operation from various tribal groups in its construction. It was built at a time when society was changing and an hereditory elite group was emerging to rule the communities.

Two Vases found during excavations at Arbor Low (Bateman)

HOW DID LEEK'S EARLY FARMERS LIVE?

LOCATION

When our Leek ancestors first came to settle here they would have been looking for a site that gave them a continuous supply of pure water, shelter, timber for housing and most important of all, fertile ground which was easy to work. Leek had all of these things.

Looking first at the location. It is likely that the first farmers who built 'Cock Low' chose that particular site because it had a light, southery aspect and the high, gritstone moors to the north gave shelter from the biting, winter winds. Leek then also had many more natural springs flowing through the ground rocks than it has today; the water supply would have been easily accessible. The near-by River Churnet provided fish, waterfowl and perhaps transport for simple wooden boats, while the river banks gave a supply of reeds for thatching houses. Trees grew almost everywhere, especially down in the valleys, and woods and trees provided natural wild food, fuel for fires, solid timber for building and wood for the carving out of weapons and tools such as bowels and ladels. However, because wood rots quickly archaeological finds of man-made wooden objects are rare. Finally, the soil was light, sandy and there was natural drainage for excess ground water down into the Churnet Valley. All in all, an ideal spot to set up a farming community.

HOUSES

Although we have no actual archaeological evidence (except for the burial mounds) as to what the Leek settlement looked like, as ploughing and human activity throughout the centuries destroyed almost all that exisited, we can draw on findings from other Neolithic/Bronze/Iron Age settlements that have been carefully excavated - for the general settlement pattern would have been similar throughout the country.

The circular houses built by our early Leek ancestors would have been relatively small, but well built, using oakwood with a reed thatching. They had a cental hearth or pit for cooking. Within the Peak District, rectangular buildings from this time have also been excavated. These had internal divisions and more than one fire pit, and perhaps held an extended family group. The village sited at 'Cock Low', like others at that time, would have been small. The families living there would form a clan with a leader.

The buildings stood either singly or as part of a group. Each house or group of houses would have its own small yard or garden. Some may have been surrounded by an enclosure bank.

FARMING AND FOOD

These early farmers probably practised all year-round, mixed farming. They began to adapt and change the landscape to their own farming needs by clearing and coppicing woodland, as well as cultivating the ground; their legacy is still with us today. We know that wheat, barley, peas, beans and herbs were likely to have been grown in the surrounding fields, which were ploughed using simple wooden ploughs drawn by men or oxen. The wheat was used to make bread. Over time the farming tools improved with the introduction of metals. By the Bronze Age, bronze chisel edged impliments were being used for breaking up and hoeing the soil, along with the older flint edged tools such as sickles.

The people also knew how to breed and keep pigs, cattle and sheep in wooden enclosures. These animals were grazed on the higher grassland and in the copiced woods, which provided nuts, wild berries and fruit. It was around this time that farmers began to grow cultivated apple and fruit trees in enclosures, rather than just gathering them from the wild. It is also believed that the local clans gathered together at the time of ploughing and harvest for feasting and ceremonies.

Rivers were an important feature of everyday life, and we know that carved wooden boats with paddles were used not only for travelling along rivers such as the Churnet but also for fishing. Fish were caught using spears with fluted, leafshaped heads and bone fishing hooks.

During these early centuries new settlers, who were farmers and herdsmen, were moving in from the West around Macclesfield. These people brought with them improved farming and grazing methods for animals, which were quickly adopted by the local clans who came into contact with them. There was a racial mixing of the old population and the new.

Evidence suggests that these early systems of farming would have been in use right up to the late Iron Age and early centuries of the Roman invasions. This fact may well apply to the farming community in Leek. Also from the evidence of the number of burial mounds within the Staffordshire Moorlands it seems likely that there were many farming clans living within this area during those past centuries.

CLOTHING AND JEWELLERY

The keeping of sheep meant a ready supply of wool. The main item of clothing for the farmers of Leek would have been a flax or woollen tunic with a V neck and a woven, woollen hat. The women wore long woollen dresses dyed different colours using herbs boiled in water. Sheep skins were used for outer clothing and bedding. Sewing was done with carved bone and wooden needles.

In time the bone and wooden jewellery was replaced as gold, copper and bronze were introduced. In those days, the gold and bronze a man possessed marked out his status within the clan.

The Chieftain was the leader of the clan. He was the most important and richest male. His cloak was held together with bronze pins, while his tunic was decorated with gold capped buttons.

WEAPONS OF WAR

The Chieftain's most prized and important possession was his bronze axe and sword. It was once thought that the Neolithic/Bronze Age was a relatively peaceful time; however, a recent archaeolgical study by Sheffield University has shown that Bronze Age man fought vicious tribal battles using spears and rapiers. War and the threat of

26

war were part of every day life, even no doubt for the clans living around Leek. Seven large and dramatic remains of later Iron Age defensive forts still exist today in Staffordshire. Their huge ramparts and deep ditches are very impressive to see. They are quite sophisticated structures and would have served as a protective focal point for those living in the surrounding areas.

Two separate halves of a Bronze Age sword were found buried on two hills at opposite sides of a valley at Hanford, Stoke-on-Trent. This sword can now be seen in Hanley Museum. Why this sword was cut cleanly in two and then buried in this way can only be guessed at or imagined. It does go to show, however, that Stoke-on-Trent does have a history that well pre-dates the Industrial Revolution. Much harm and environmental damage has been done to the area by Man's activities, so any archaelogical finds, such as the Bronze Age sword, should be treasured and preserved by the people of Stoke-on-Trent.

Bronze Age sword of the type found by Bateman & one found in Stoke-on Trent

The craftsmen who worked in gold in those past times made fine intricate jewellery, some of which was decorated with tiny birds and animals. They even crafted portraits of people. The women wore necklaces and bracelets of gold, bronze and amber. Amber is actually resin from trees which grew in pre-historic forests. It is often found washed up on beaches. Many 'pebbles' of amber contain mummified insects from the time of the dinosaurs. This fascinated our ancient ancestors and they believed amber to be a magical stone. Status based on bronze and gold soon led to the development of the first class structure within the farming clans.

LANGUAGE

The Bronze Age people of Leek used what is now called, 'The Old European Language'. They spoke with a 'Brythonic' dialect. They also used a system of writing called, 'Ogham'. It was formed by a series of straight lines stemming from a central vertical line, and was utilised for inscriptions on stones. There are no examples of it in England. Although Ogham worked for stone carving, it was of little use for everyday writing. In fact, very little remains in England of the language of these early people.

First the invading Romans, then the Anglo-Saxon/Vikings did a very thorough job of wiping out almost every trace of both the language and culture of those early Britons.

Still, all is not lost for us as place-name historians now assume (after careful analysis) that the name of the River Churnet was 'given' by our 'celtic' Leek ancestors, as no connection can be made to later languages - but we have little idea what the word 'churnet' means. Some other local place-names also remain, based on natural features. One of these is 'Combes Valley'. 'Combe' is an old Celtic word for 'deep valley'.

The name 'Leek', however, does not come from that time; it originated in the Anglo-Saxon/Viking era. This is discussed in the later Anglo-Saxon chapter.

TRADE & TRAVEL

It is an amazing fact that Britain was already known about in places like the Lebanon as long ago as the Bronze/Iron Age. Phoenician traders were coming from the Far East to these shores trading for tin. It is also a fact that our ancestors at that time were using a series of trackways for trade and travel which dated back to earlier pre-historic times. These people were actually far more sophisticated, both socially and culturally, than previously thought.

❖   ❖   ❖   ❖

We can side-track, so to speak, for a moment   in order to examine the old story which said that Jesus Christ came as a young child to Glastonbury, in Somerset, England with his Uncle, Joseph of Arimathea.   Joseph was said to be a tin-trader who regularly travelled to England to buy tin for export back to his homeland. It is this story which gave rise to the famous Glastonbury legends regarding the Holy Grail (the cup used at 'The Last Supper' by Jesus which is said to be buried at Glastonbury) and the famous Thorn Tree which was supposed to have grown when Joseph of Arimathea planted a wooden staff, cut from a thorn tree in the Middle East, into the ground at Glastonbury.
The well-known hymn, 'Jerusalem' celebrates this story, when it says, "And did those feet (meaning Jesus) in ancient times, walk upon England's mountains green?"

Legends and old stories often have a grain of truth hidden deep inside them, and one can easily see how this story of Jesus came about, for it is based on the true fact that the British/Far Eastern tin trade had been going on for centuries before Jesus was born. The tin traders would have used ancient trackways to transport their metal.

❖   ❖   ❖   ❖

THE LEEK TRACKWAY

The Leek Moorlands had its own pre-historic trackway which was used and utilised in later centuries, and which can still be traced today. From its alignment it seems that its route touched points on the landscape where ancient ceremonial sites were located.

We can pick up its line at Waterhouses, nr. Leek, then at 'Waterfall Cross' an ancient pre-historic landmark where three ways meet. The track runs on a line to Bottom House, (past Standing Stone's Farm) follows a footpath to Lower Lady Meadows, then goes down to 'Combes Brook' (Celtic Place-name). It next joins the Ashbourne Road to Cook's Lane and then goes to Bradnop and "Low Hill" (site of burial mound). The track passes right through Leek itself up to an escarpment known as 'The Cloud' (the hill behind which the Midsummer sun sets twice). It then passes 'The Bridestones' (the Neolithic Burial Chamber) and descends down into the Cheshire Plain.

It was trackways such as this which allowed trade and communications between the clans. Polished axes from this time have been discovered in the Leek Moorland's area, within the Peak District and in other parts of the country. These axes were commonly made of hard igneous rocks - and the source of this rock is the Lake District, Cumbria and North Wales. It is believed that a Neolithic 'factory' for axes exisisted at Great Langdale in the Lake District, and that these axes were carried to all parts of the country. Several hundred such axes have been found within the Peak Park, and one of them originated from Northern Ireland.

A glass bead from Egypt was found in a Bronze Age burial mound close to Stanton Moor, and further evidence has shown that trade was being carried on between the early Britons and the eastern Mediterranean over 3,500 years ago. In fact luxury goods were being carried along the ancient trackways from sea-ports into the very heart of the Peak District itself.

Historians believe that the trackways were also **PILGRIM ROUTES. Our ancient Leek ancestors used them to visit henges or ceremonial sites at certain times of the year.** If you follow along the line of the old trackway which runs through Leek, it will eventually bring you to the previously mentioned famous **'Arbor Low '**, then onto **'Minninglow', 'Stoney Low', 'Green Low'** and many other such ancient sites.

The early farming clans of Leek and its Moorlands continued to live and farm for many, many centuries, undisturbed except perhaps for inter-clan warfare which would have mainly revolved around ownership of land. However, as with all things, it could not last. Across the deep blue waters, which divided Britain from mainland Europe, a mighty foreign power had its sights set on this little island and its natural wealth. Life was about to change dramatically.

'Nine Stones' Neolithic Stone Circle at 'Hart Hill'

'PAX ROMANS'

In 55 BC Julius Caesar landed on the eastern coast of these islands. He fought a number of battles, then left. Almost a century later, in 43 AD, Claudius led the conquest of 'BRITAINNIA'. The Romans were to remain here for another 400 years.

The effects were tremendous. In under 40 years most of Britain, including the Staffordshire Moorlands, came under the rule of Rome or 'PAX ROMANS', which translated means, 'ROMAN PEACE'.

It is known that the Roman army entered the general area of the Peak District and the Staffordshire Moorlands in the late 70's AD.   The land was occupied in order to secure the advance of the Roman armies which were by now moving further and further north. Total control in this region came swiftly and peacefully.

The Roman soldiers were extremely well disciplined and well-equipped. They were experts in the art of war and securing the peace.. In a very short time, they had overcome all opposition from the Britons and Rome controlled almost every aspect of life. A single Roman Legion was made up of more than 3,000 men. Every soldier was skilled in the building of roads, river-crossings and bridges, as well as the art of warfare. They could march 20 miles a day and were almost totally self-sufficient. Sometimes male Britons were drafted in to join the army as auxiliaries.

COMMUNICATIONS

It would have been an advanced Roman Legion that built the Roman Road that passes through Leek on its way to the ancient spar town of 'Buxton'.

The Leek to Buxton Road crossed the River Churnet at 'Wall Bridge'. It was constructed so as to avoid the flood plain of the river on one side and the steepness of the rolling sandstone hills on the other.

The road or 'AGGER' was constructed to the same design as every other road built by the Roman armies. It was not likely to have been a major road and was proably no wider than 16 feet, whereas major roads were up to 40 feet wide. But it was well constructed. In the peaty areas drainage ditches were dug on either side. Between these ditches large stones were laid. These were then covered with finer material. Some parts of the road would have been paved like a wide pavement. Like every road built by the invading armies, it more or less followed a straight line. It would have formed part of the intricate network of 180,000 miles of paved roads which connected all the Romano-British towns and ports.

Cross section of a Roman Road in Peak District.

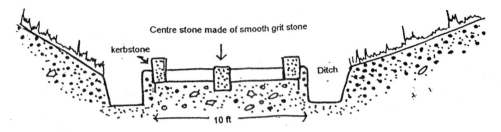

Centre stone made of smooth grit stone

kerbstone

Ditch

10 ft

THE LINE TAKEN BY THE LEEK ROMAN ROAD

The Leek Roman road was not only built to improve communication, it was also a military road and was part of a system linking military forts. If any trouble or fighting occured, Roman soldiers could easily be despatched between forts to the trouble spot.

It is a fact that the old Bronze/Iron Age 'lows' continued to be used for religious burials by the Romano/British for a while after the Roman occupation - And new Romano/British 'lows' were sometimes built alongside the new Roman Roads.

The Romans also used the existing Neolithic/Bronze/Iron Age burial mounds as sighting points for the building of their communication network.

At the time the Leek to Buxton road was being constructed, the skyline of the Staffordshire Moorlands would have been full of old 'barrows' and 'lows'.

We can actually trace the line of the Roman road.

Its route from Buxton leads south-west and follows a series of straight lines along the modern road, the A53. The Ordnance Survey Map - 1inch marks out the Roman Road section longside Ramshaw Rocks on the Roaches. The line then carries on to Leek. It continues down the present Buxton Road, passing the 'Moss Rose'. It follows the old route into Leek traced by the lane called 'The Organ Ground'. It next goes down Fountain Street, along Derby Street on a route towards Strangman Street - Here it passed close by the Bronze Age Burial Mound of 'Cock Low'. Dropping down the slope, it next followed the line of 'The Walks', with a section cut off by the 20th century railway line. It then ran along Newcastle Road to 'Wall Bridge'. The Roman engineers made certain they avoided the natural flood plain, while that particular crossing point over the Churnet was

The most likely route through Leek of the Leek to Buxton road built by the Roman army in their advance northwards.

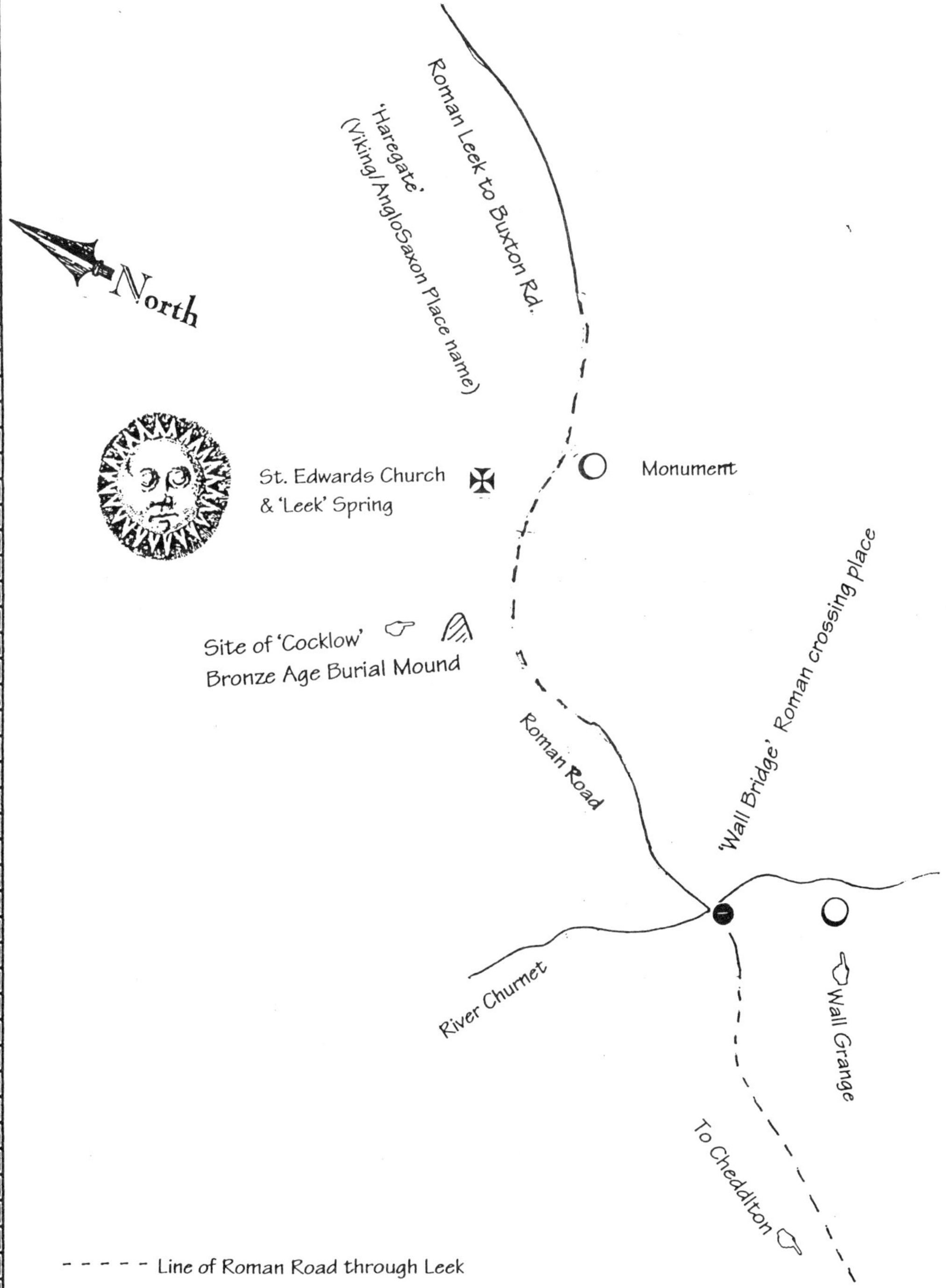

North

Roman Leek to Buxton Rd.

'Haregate' (Viking/AngloSaxon Place name)

St. Edwards Church & 'Leek' Spring

Monument

Site of 'Cocklow' Bronze Age Burial Mound

Roman Road

'Wall Bridge' Roman crossing place

River Churnet

Wall Grange

To Cheddlton

- - - - - Line of Roman Road through Leek

chosen because it was the narrowest part of the river valley.

The ancient road continued on to 'Wall Grange', then 'Cheddleton' and eventually 'Blythe Bridge', before heading South. In 1962, excavations made by the City of Stoke-on-Trent Archaeology Society were able to confirm the general line of the Roman Road someway south of Leek.

ROMAN PLACE NAMES

Attention must be drawn here to the Place-names of,

'WALL BRIDGE' and 'WALL GRANGE'.

These two places are located at the edge of Leek alongside the River Churnet and close to the point where the Roman Road crossed the river.

Ekwall, the famous and respected Place-Name historian points out in his writings that, 'EVIDENCE OF ROMAN OCCUPATION AND ROMAN REMAINS HAVE ALWAYS BEEN DISCOVERED IN PLACES WHICH CARRY THE PLACE-NAME, 'WALL'.

Can we confidently assume that Leek is no exception to this rule - that somewhere in the 'Wall Bridge', 'Wall-Grange' area there was a Roman presence? The answer is, Yes!

We can consider the likely possibility that the Romans built within the vicinity a fort to regulate the crossings over the River Churnet at 'Wall Bridge'. It is a fact that Leek is 12 miles from Buxton. It is also a fact that the Romans sited their forts at 12 mile intervals along their roads. Buxton had a military fort, so we could expect one at Leek. At these forts there would be a bath-house, stables and living quarters. Sometimes there were ramparts with ditches, and possibly two or three entrance gates. Some Roman forts in Staffordshire were over 30 acres in area, but the one at Leek would have been somewhat smaller.

There is also the possibility that a Roman Villa or farm was also situated in the vicinity which serviced the fort. Romano/British villas were profit-making farms. They could be the size of an average modern house or a large country house. These villas were usually connected with the native Romano/British rather than immigrants from Rome itself. They were owned and run by the Cheiftens of the old British tribes. Some villas would have at first been simple affairs, but as time went on and the old ways were forgotten, verandas, courtyards and bath houses were added. The villas were built of stone and timber, with Roman colonnades at the front. They often had mosaic floors and pavements. The walls were brightly decorated with scenes from either Roman or Greek legends. Slaves or crofters worked the land. It is known that the population of Brittainia benefited a great deal from Roman Rule. Income increased as local farming clans supplied food and goods to the Roman forts and garrisons.

To add weight to the theory that a fort existed in the 'Wall-Bridge', 'Wall-Grange' areas, we need to refer to the Medieaval Dieulacrest Charters from Dieulacrest Abbey. This charter gives the title of the road leading to 'Wall-Bridge' as the,

'Via castelia'.

This translated from the original Latin means,

'The Road to the Castle'.

This definitely does not refer to the town of Newcastle, but tells us that as early as 1214 AD there must still have been a stone building of great note standing within the vicinity.

Also legal documents from the time of Dieulacres Abbey clearly refer to the area at 'Wall Bridge' as 'Le Wall' and 'Wal juxta Leek', which translated means, 'The Wall near (next to) Leek'. We have to remember that the Old English word, *wall*' at that time did not actually mean 'a wall' but referred to 'a stone built fortification' or a defensive wall as in, 'town and city walls' or walls surrounding castles and forts. It was only during much later times that the word 'wall' came to be used in a more general sense.

In the 1200's only very important buildings such as castles and churches were built of stone - everything else was built of timber. After the Romans had left these shores people living in the so-called 'Dark-Ages' described the Roman stone buildings left behind as, 'THE WORKS OF GIANTS'. This is because the classical and military architectural designs would have seemed huge and 'castle-like'.

It is worth recalling here that historians and archaeologists in Chesterton spent many years looking for the remains of a Roman fort they knew had existed in the town. They eventually found it under a place called, "CASTLE STREET" .
If only they had taken careful note of place-name evidence, they would have located the fort much sooner.

The 'Waste' and the 'Mount', which are both high points above the town, would have given a good 'military' view across the valley and beyond - And close to them we find the notable place-name, that of 'HARE-GATE'. This very ancient name means,

34

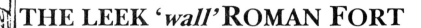

THE LEEK 'wall' ROMAN FORT

Historical and place-name evidence clearly denotes the location of a Roman military stone fort in the 'Wall Grange' area of Leek during the Romano British period. This fort formed part of the military communications road network and regulated crossings over the River Churnet at the 'wall-bridge' site. In the early days it would have been a purely defensive building containing accommodation & sleeping quarters for the soldiers, plus stables for horses.

The illustration on the right shows how the Gate Way to the Leek Roman Fort would have looked during the Roman era. There would also have been defensive ramparts topped by wooden walk-ways and look-out/signalling towers. The living quarters & stables were built inside the outer walls. Various other 'service' buildings would have been added on later as the local population became Romanised.

As Roman rule became firmly established the fort doubled as a wayside 'inn' or resting place for travellers and merchants using the Leek section of the Roman road. It would almost certainly have been serviced by an on-site farming villa owned by a Romano-British Chieftain & his extended family. Along with its adjoining road, the fort brought increased wealth and prosperity to the local population. The whole area should now be given special protection from any further development so that important and irreplaceable archaeological evidence is not destroyed by developers, as it has been in many other parts of Leek.

The road from Leek to Buxton, once a Roman Road. Close by is 'Haregate', ancient Saxon/Viking place-name meaning 'soldier's road' (Roman).

'Wall Grange', most likely site of Roman fort/agricultural villa connected to the Roman Road which crossed the River Churnet at Wall Bridge, Leek.

'SOLDIER'S ROAD' and the word 'GATE' was used by the later Vikings (who settled in the Staffordshire Moorlands) to describe important military roads which had existed much earlier. In the case of 'Hare-gate', this most definately refers to the Roman road to Buxton and the fact that it was a road used by a well organised military force.

We have to stop here and wonder just what important archaeological evidence has been, **and may be lost**, to development and the building of houses at 'Hare-gate', 'The Mount' and 'The Waste'. It is crucial that before any development ever takes place in an ancient town like Leek, a proper archaeological survey is carried out. This should include ground and air surveys. If there is any doubt, or the possibility exists of historical evidence being destroyed, then it is better that no development takes place.

BUXTON - 'AQUAE ARNEMETIAE'

Although Buxton is 12 miles from Leek, it would have been an important town for the Romano/British of the Leek Moorlands.

Buxton, which is a later Anglo-Saxon name, was called 'AQUAE ARNEMETIAE' by the Romans. 'Arnemetia' was the name of the patron goddess of the Buxton Spring. It means, '*She who dwelt over against the sacred grove*'. In the 1590's a statue was found bearing the word, 'ARNE', which was the beginning of the word 'Arnemetiae'. This was mistaken for the name 'ANNE', so today that same spring or well in the Crescent is called, St. Anne's Well'.

The Roman fort was sited on the high ground of Higher Buxton. The actual lead-lined baths built during the Roman occupation could still be seen in 1780. They were close to the present day St. Anne's well. It is likely that these warm spa waters were already being used by the early Britons before the Roman invasion. Buxton (Aquae Arnemetiae) was under military occupation during the early days of the conquest. Later as Roman rule became established, it was used as a social spa. Soldiers, officials and Romano/British citizens would visit the town for rest and holidays - no doubt some of them passed through Leek on their journey there.

ROMAN RULE

Were the Ancient Britons living within the Leek Moorlands amazed or afraid at their first sighting of a Roman Legion marching into the area? We can't be sure - but

TRADE AND MARKETS

The Romans brought with them a new order, a more civilised way of living - Not only in the classical style of building with fine decoration, plumbing and under-floor heating, but classical art, sculpture, music, theatre, ballet and poetry. They imported toothbrushes, perfumes, ivory, glassware, beautiful clothing and jewellery. It was a refined type of living never before seen in these islands.

Across the network of roads, carts and pack-horses brought lead and silver from Derbyshire- also tin, gold and salt from Cheshire. Millstone Grit from the Pennines was used in corn mills or was exported back to Rome. Fine pottery and French wines called 'posca' for the troops and the silver coinage 'denarius' were imported, as was papyrus for books and documents. Along with Roman lamps, came olive oils from Spain

Although we have no actual archaeological evidence as yet to draw upon, it is likely that Leek was already a small market trading area in Roman times. The Romano/British held fairs and markets which attracted people from a wide area. Such markets were held close to the site of a Roman Road for ease of access and travel. Associated with these markets were sanctuaries or 'holy places'. If Leek did indeed hold such a market, it would most likely have been located close to the site of the 'Old Cattle Market' or the present day 'Smithfield Shopping Centre'.
When the day finally arrives for the much needed demolition of the 'Smithfield Centre', perhaps the new shops could be designed in a classical Roman style in celebration of Leek's early Roman Road.

The Roman market area had its own deity who would bless the buying and selling of goods. There would have been a small temple or shrine surrounded by venerated trees such as the Yew. Although these shrines were very common around the countryside - they actually formed one of the most characteristic features of the landscape in rural Roman Britain - very few have remained due to post-Roman building and development.
Theatre, fairs and festivals would also be held at these places- and at special times of the year the goddess of the shrine would be crowned with a wreath of flowers.

A Selection from Roman finds made by Bateman in the Staffordshire Moorlands

lExcavation Report – " On the 9th. September we opened a mound 9 yards across near Thor's Cave, Wetton. ..Near the centre about a foot below the surface we found two very curious vessels. ..one which may be styled a bronze pan or kettle, 4 inches high 6 inches diameter, with a slender iron bow like a bucket handle. It has been first cast and then hammered …
– Romano - British.

Finds – August 7th 1852. Plain bronze ring fibula without pin found interred with skeleton , Wetton, Staffs. June 24th. 1848. Bronze heart shaped fibula with coiled spring to head of pin, perfect (condition). 2 ½ inches long. Found in barrow at Greenfield, Castern, Staffs.- Below right is an example of a similar fibula found in Monyash, Derbyshire,

Romano-British Broad Iron Knife. Found Nov. 1850. Much corroded, with the original stag's horn handle still attached. Found in Boroughs, Wetton, Staffordshire Along with a small slip of bronze (metal) with a hole at each end.

TRADE AND MARKETS

The Romans brought with them a new order, a more civilised way of living - Not only in the classical style of building with fine decoration, plumbing and under-floor heating, but classical art, sculpture, music, theatre, ballet and poetry. They imported toothbrushes, perfumes, ivory, glassware, beautiful clothing and jewellery. It was a refined type of living never before seen in these islands.

Across the network of roads, carts and pack-horses brought lead and silver from Derbyshire- also tin, gold and salt from Cheshire. Millstone Grit from the Pennines was used in corn mills or was exported back to Rome. Fine pottery and French wines called 'posca' for the troops and the silver coinage 'denarius' were imported, as was papyrus for books and documents. Along with Roman lamps, came olive oils from Spain

Although we have no actual archaeological evidence as yet to draw upon, it is likely that Leek was already a small market trading area in Roman times. The Romano/British held fairs and markets which attracted people from a wide area. Such markets were held close to the site of a Roman Road for ease of access and travel. Associated with these markets were sanctuaries or 'holy places'. If Leek did indeed hold such a market, it would most likely have been located close to the site of the 'Old Cattle Market' or the present day 'Smithfield Shopping Centre'.
When the day finally arrives for the much needed demolition of the 'Smithfield Centre', perhaps the new shops could be designed in a classical Roman style in celebration of Leek's early Roman Road.

The Roman market area had its own deity who would bless the buying and selling of goods. There would have been a small temple or shrine surrounded by venerated trees such as the Yew. Although these shrines were very common around the countryside - they actually formed one of the most characteristic features of the landscape in rural Roman Britain - very few have remained due to post-Roman building and development.
Theatre, fairs and festivals would also be held at these places- and at special times of the year the goddess of the shrine would be crowned with a wreath of flowers.

A Selection from Roman finds made by Bateman in the Staffordshire Moorlands

lExcavation Report – " On the 9th. September we opened a mound 9 yards across near Thor's Cave, Wetton. ..Near the centre about a foot below the surface we found two very curious vessels. ..one which may be styled a bronze pan or kettle, 4 inches high 6 inches diameter, with a slender iron bow like a bucket handle. It has been first cast and then hammered …
– Romano – British.

Finds – August 7th 1852. Plain bronze ring fibula without pin found interred with skeleton , Wetton, Staffs. June 24th. 1848. Bronze heart shaped fibula with coiled spring to head of pin, perfect (condition). 2 ½ inches long. Found in barrow at Greenfield, Castern, Staffs.- Below right is an example of a similar fibula found in Monyash, Derbyshire,

Romano-British Broad Iron Knife.
Found Nov. 1850. Much corroded, with the original stag's horn handle still attached. Found in Boroughs, Wetton, Staffordshire Along with a small slip of bronze (metal) with a hole at each end.

RELIGION

Religion played a great part in the life of the Romano/British. The Romans, who were at first pagans, were quite tolerant of other religions - the only Religions they would not tolerate under any circumstances were those that included cannibalism and human sacrifice. This is why the Romans at first objected to Christianity. They saw the taking of bread and wine, which is supposed to be the body and blood of Christ, as a form of cannibalism. The Romans also wiped out, almost over-night, the Druid priests which existed here at the time of the Roman invasion. The Druids were in fact late-comers on to the British Religious scene, and they had no connection what-so-ever to the building of Stone Henge. Many Druid Priests were pursued over-land by the Romans into Angelsey, where they had a holy centre. They were completely surrounded, then every one of the priests was slaughtered by the Roman soldiers. The reason they were so ruthlessly dealt with by the Romans was not because they indulged in human sacrifice, which they did not (this was a piece of later Romantic nonsense), but because they gave political guidance and inspiration to the Early British clan leaders who fought against the Roman invaders.

The Romano/British were expected to worship the Roman Emperor as a God. But in those times there were many Gods and Godlings.
Shrines to the Goddess Silvanus, who was the stream Goddess connected to hunting, have been found in cloughs in the Pennine Moorlands.
Ialonus was the God of the Meadowland, Suleviae was a Gaelic Mother Goddess; Fortuna guarded against evil, Dea Hammia was the God of Archers and Hercules replaced the local Celtic God, Segomo. Shrines to such gods would have, at first, been raised by the Commanders of the Roman Forts, such as the one at 'Wall-Bridge'. In time they were adopted by the local population.

ROMAN FINDS

There have been a number of Roman finds in the area. A Roman sandal and lamp were found at Smythy Farm, Leek Frith. Leek-Frith was once part of the ancient Parish of Leek.

At Wetton, a Romano/British lead mining village was excavated. Finds included Roman glass, a bronze ring and beads. There were also Roman coins from the Emperors Gallienus - AD 253, Tetricius AD 268 and Constantine AD 306. Also discoverd at that site was a bronze pin with a hoof-shaped head, a lead collar and a heart shaped bronze fibula enamelled blue, yellow and green. This is thought to be late Roman.

The bodies of pre-Christian Romans were burnt after death. The ashes were placed in earthenware urns, similar to those of the earlier Britons. Roman burials have actually been found in the top layers of earlier Bronze Age mounds.

Roman Burial Lows have been located at BLORE, ILAM, WETTON & WATERHOUSES nr. Leek. Thomas Bateman wrote a rather amusing report of an excavation in ALSTONEFILED in the Staffordshire Moorlands; he wrote,

On the 21st of June, 1845 an attempt was made to open a large barrow near Alstonefield, called 'Steep Low' measuring about fifty yards in diameter, and about fifteen feet in central elevation, which is constructed almost entirely of loose stones. It was found on reaching the place that some of the neighbouring villagers had already, in a vain search after imaginary treasure, found near the apex of the mound, the body of a Romanized Briton, extended on his back, accompanied by an iron spear-head, a lance head and knife of the same placed near the head, and three Roman coins in third brass, namely of Constantine the Great, one of Lectricus, the other illegible from the friction of the sand-paper applied by the finder in the delusive hope of making evident its golden character. They also found some pieces of a highly-ornamented drinking cup..All the antiquities discovered by those enterprising individuals were ceded to the writer, on their being reimbursed for their labour and loss of time…On continuing my excavation there was discovered, close to where the spears were found, a small stud or circular ornament of copal amber, perforated with a double hole at the back for attachment.

At Cauldon Low, nr. Leek pottery from the late second and third century, plus a Roman Crucible were discovered. These are now in Derby Museum

We know, from excavations done under the aegis of the City Museum, Stoke-on-Trent in 1955, that a Roman Pottery and workshop existed in Trent Vale. Here was made Roman lamp-holders, platters, bowls, wine flagons and cooking pots. No other such pottery workshop has been found in the North Midlands, so it must have been a very important site, providing pots and ware for a wide area of the country, including the Staffordshire Moorlands and Buxton. Some of the pottery fragments found there were beautifully decorated with dolphins, leaves, rosettes, leafy festoons in the shape of an arcade and Roman figures. Some of the pots were either in rich brown or pinkish clay. Roman coins, bronze studs and a bronze brooch had also been found earlier on the site.

The Romans imported a great deal of finely-made, brilliant red Samian pottery.

from Italy. All excavations on Roman farms, villas and towns in Britain have yielded this type of pottery. Egyption pottery was also imported, and this had words such as, 'VIVATIS' which means, 'LONG LIFE TO YOU' etched on it.

A Roman coin hoard was found in the 1700's at Friar Moor, nr. Leek. With this particular find in mind we can look back at the Anglo-Saxon Chronicles written in Saxon times which states that,

'In 410 the Goths broke into Rome and Roman rule declined in Britain. The Romans in Britain gathered all the gold-hoards that were in Britain. Some they hid in the earth, so that no man might find them. Some they took to Gaul'.

Was the hoard of coins found on Friar Moor left behind by someone fleeing back to Rome or by some local Romano/Briton? We have no way of knowing. However, we know that the inner territories of Rome remained intact for a while. Roman coinage was still being produced in these islands as late as the 4th. century AD. New Roman villas were also still being built in Britain in 369 AD.

In 367 AD Hadrian's Wall in the north of the country was over-run by the Picts, and by 409 AD, Roman rule in these islands had all but ended. Once the Romans had left, the pages of history turned and a new chapter began for the people of the Staffordshire Moorlands.

This is an early photograph of a Roman Altar with a Latin inscription. (A History of Cheshire C.E. Kelsy) It was found in Chester (Roman name 'Deva') Chester was an important military Roman city that contained many fine & important Roman buildings. The first Roman soldiers to arrive there defeated the local British tribe called the 'Cornavii'. A second tribe, which occupied the high hilly areas to the north-east, along the Pennine Chain (and possibly the Staffordshire. Moorlands) called the 'Brigantes' were far more warlike. They resisted for a number of years before being overcome by the might of the Roman army under their General Ostorrius Scapula. (They were not thoroughly subdued until the reign of Vespasian AD 69-79). A tribe called the 'Cangi' occupied Cannock Chase in Staffordshire.

The Leek AngloSaxons and Vikings

Photograph by Helen Ball

A stone carving of the English Anglo Saxon God called 'ING' or the 'GREEN MAN'. His Rune Sign was

THE COMING OF THE ANGLO SAXONS
AND VIKINGS TO LEEK

The Roman Legions did not leave Britain because of the invasions from the North. They were actually recalled as a result of the changing political system back in Rome, where the Generals were fighting amongst themselves. In 410 AD the leaders of the Romano/British sent a letter to the Emperor Honorius asking for help in defending their island home. Honorius wrote back to say, they would have to defend themselves.

Until the year 440 AD Romano/British leaders such as Vortigern managed to keep the invading Picts at bay using paid Anglo-Saxon mercenaries from Germany. These Saxons, under their commanders, Hengesat and Horsa, came across in ships and helped the Romano/British to drive out the Picts. Hengesat and Horsa, however, were not slow to recognise a good thing when they saw it. They sent a message back to N. Germany to say, 'The land here is good and fertile, the Romano British can't defend themselves'. Some Anglo-Saxons settlers had been living quietly in Britain for some time - But once Hengest and Horsa realised the land was there for the taking, it was only a matter of time before a full-scale Anglo/Saxon invasion began

Life for the Romano/British people of the Leek Moorlands probably did not change too dramtically once the Roman Legions had left. Most of the imports and exports to and from Rome would have declined. Although the Roman Road through Leek was no longer maintained as well as in the past, it would have continued to be used for trade and travel.
Roman Aquae Arnemetiae (Buxton), however, went into slow decline. The population moved from the lower parts of the town, where the baths were situated, to the higher more easily defended areas.

The invading Saxon armies continued to fight westward across the country, but unlike the previous Romans who were efficient and organised , these new invaders were individual war bands who were intent on setting up their own individual kingdoms.

The first settlement of the Midlands was led by the Saxon leader, Crida. The Saxons probably arrived in the Staffordshire Moorlands in the late Sixth century. They found their way here by using rivers and the existing Roman roads. We know that by 700 AD there was a successful tribe of Germanic Anglo-Saxons living north of the Leek

Moorlands. These were 'The Pecsietna' - they lived in a Saxon Tribal area of land.

There is no evidence as such to suggest that the coming of the Saxons to this area resulted in warfare. There was more likely to have been a peaceful integration with the local population who had, by now, discarded much of their Roman way of life.

Leek and its Moorlands soon became part of the Saxon Kingdom of Mercia, which was a collection of smaller tribes.

The Anglo-Saxon period lasted for six hundred years, <u>and it was during this time that the town of 'Leek' acquired its name.</u>

So, just what kind of people were our Saxon Leek Ancestors?

In order to answer this question we need to look briefly at their cultural, religious and politcal background.

To begin with, the Anglo-Saxons originated from the Germanic tribes on the European Continent and they brought with them their own culture, heroic traditions, legends, and folk-lore.

They quite literally and most ruthlessly wiped out the traditions and language of the Britons they found here. Their arrival was to herald the exact moment in history when England became the country we all know and recognise today. The Englishness of our character, our social structures, our legends, traditions, place-names and most of all our English language found its roots at that time.

The Anglo-Saxons called this island, **'ENGLALAND'**. It was a country already well endowed with post-Roman towns, settlements and many farmsteads. However, it was the Saxons who instigated the development of the typical English village with its central place of worship surrounded by clusters of houses, halls and other buildings. The main towns and villages, such as Leek, were firmly established during this time.

Seven Saxon Kingdoms were set-up. Leek was set in the central Kingdom of Mercia. These seven kingdoms, each with its own King, struggled to gain military supremacy over the rest - In time Mercia, which had begun as a western outpost in the valleys of the rivers Trent and Dove, became an enormous Kingdom bounded on one side by the Humber and Wales on the other.

43

THE SAXON LORDS AND THEIR WARRIORS

One well known Lord was King Alfred's Grandson, Edward. For a time he ruled over Mercia and the Leek Moorlands. He, like all other Lords, had a band of followers called, **'GESITHAS'** which means, 'Companions'. The Gesithas were loyal to Edward before all others, and in return he gave them splendid gifts such as helmets, horses, spears, shields and swords. These gifts were given at a special ceremony where the Gesithas would, ' lay their hands and head on the knee of the Lord and touch his sword'. They were then allowed to sleep in the hall of Edward on 'mead-benches'. This gave them place and status. The ceremony of 'gift-giving' was a time of great feasting and speechmaking. The Anglo-Saxons were very fond of speech making, and special halls were built just for just that purpose.

If one of Edward's followers was slain, he would seek vengence, and like other Lords often led his men into battle. Edmund, again like all Saxon royalty, claimed descent from the pagan Gods. Saxon Lords and Kings had great wealth. They rode through the towns and villages with their loyal warriors, and a standard-bearer went before them. It must have been a wonderful sight to see. Saxon poets at the time described the Royal courts as having, 'gold-wrought tapestries and drinking cups of precious metals'.

SHIELD-MAIDENS - It would appear that fighting in battle was not always left solely to the men. There are references in Old English literature to women, 'wearing clothing covered with metal plates - fighting armed with long swords and shields'.

It has also been suggested by archaelogists that weapons found in some Saxon burial sites may have belonged to women. There is actually a poem from that time which describes a 'Shield-Maiden'. It says;

'Then the woman with braided hair — A sharp sword, hard in battle, and drew it from its sheath with her right hand'

illustration Saxon Village Project Wessex

We also know that King Alfred's Grandaughter, Ethelfleada, who was known as 'Our Lady of the Mercians', often went out with with the Mercian army in times of battle. Along with her brother, Edward King of Wessex, she helped to free Derby from the Vikings and established Stafford as the borough town of Staffordshire.

Some of The Saxons Kings

The Anglo-Saxon period lasted for many hundreds of years and during this time there were many Kings. Some of the names are familiar today, a great many others are not. Below is a list of some of these Kings and the dates when they ruled.

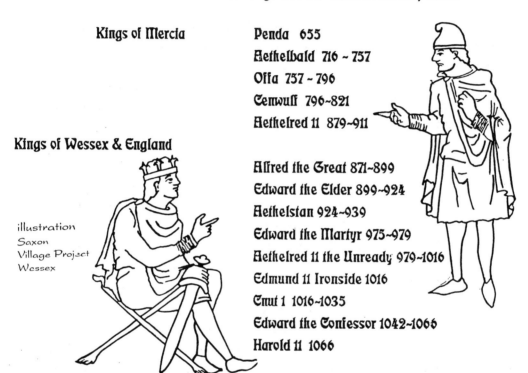

Kings of Mercia

Penda 655
Aethelbald 716 ~ 757
Offa 757 ~ 796
Cenwulf 796~821
Aethelred 11 879~911

Kings of Wessex & England

illustration
Saxon
Village Project
Wessex

Alfred the Great 871~899
Edward the Elder 899~924
Aethelstan 924~939
Edward the Martyr 975~979
Aethelred 11 the Unready 979~1016
Edmund 11 Ironside 1016
Cnut 1 1016~1035
Edward the Confessor 1042~1066
Harold 11 1066

Many of these kings were good kings, but the greatest one of all was King Alfred. Sadly, because the history of England prior to 1066 is so neglected by our education system, most people only equate King Alfred with the story of the 'burning of the cakes'. In fact, Alfred was the finest King England has ever had in the whole of its history. He was a great military leader who fought against all the odds against the Viking invasions of England and he won back the whole of the country for the English people while he reigned. He was a Christian and was well ahead of his time. He encouraged the setting up of church schools and universities. As a boy he travelled to Rome with a bodyguard of warriors. While in the ancient capital he was so impressed with classical architecture and culture that later, when he was King, he strove to bring the same high standards of civilisation to England. King Alfred had built impressive halls and royal chambers, while his craftsmen made fine and beautiful objects. He had translated into

English the great works of history and philosophy, and he also commissioned the writing of the famous Anglo-Saxon Chronicles in the 9th century. It recorded the arrival of the Anglo-Saxons in 449 and continued on for another 700 hundred years. It is one of the most important sources of information about this period of English history.

THE 'ORDINARY' PEOPLE OF SAXON ENGLAND

Below the Kings and Lords came the '*CHURL*'. He was an ordinary freeman. A Churl owned an eight-ox plough, pasture and woodland - all in all about a hundred acres which was called a, '*HIDE*'. There were also, '*GEBURS*' or peasants who owned a quarter of a hide. They kept an oxen, one cow, six sheep and seven acres of land. The Geburs worked for the Lord for two days a week, from Candlemas to Easter.

There was an even lower class of people called the, '*COTSETLAN*' or the 'Cottage dwellers'. They only owned five acres of land. Below the Cotsetlan came the Slave. The price for a Slave was one pound in coinage or six oxen. When the Saxons adopted Christianity, the Church tried to help the Slave. Under King Alfred, Slaves were allowed to buy their freedom.

WHO OWNED THE MANOR OF LEEK IN SAXON TIMES?

Almost everyone is familiar with the story of Lady Godiva riding through the streets of Coventry. However, Leek can also claim a connection with this renowed lady - for Lady Godiva's husband, The Earl of Mercia and also his son Algar, owned various Saxon estates and one of these was The Manor of Leek.

The Saxon Lords who owned Leek derived their income from those who owned farms or worked on the land. This interest was paid in the form of, '*FOOD-RENT*' rather than actual coinage, as the ordinary people did not always use money, but rather a 'barter-system'.

A special barn would have been built in Leek where the 'food-rent' was stored. This barn was most likely to have been sited between the present day St. Edward's Church and the Market Square. The rent paid to the Lord would have been given in the form of grain, vegetables, honey, sheep and goats, animal fleeces etc.

There was also a Saxon Manor house built on the present site of the Red Lion in the Market Square where Lord's such as Algar and his father, would come with their Warriors and *SHIREREEVE* or Sheriff to collect their dues. This would be a regular event, and the Lord would stay for maybe a week at a time.

We know from the '**Domsday Book**', that the Manor of Leek had twenty eight households. This only records the actual number of men or 'households' with its farmland and woodland. It does not document the women, children, the extended family units including the old and dependent relatives. It also does not record the workers who toiled on the land for the landowner.

The residents of Leek, like all other Saxons, would have jealously guarded their village, so much so, that any stranger approaching Leek was expected by law to blow a hunting horn to announce his coming, or shout out in a loud voice telling his name and business. If he did not do this he was in great danger of being set upon and killed. This was because the possibility of attack from outsiders or invaders was always present

'QUEEN OF THE MOORLANDS'

Even as early as Saxon times, Leek was the largest and most important settlement in the whole of the Staffordshire Moorlands. Then, as now it was 'Queen of the Moorlands'. It formed the nucleus in both trading and farming for the surrounding rural population.

CHANGES IN LANGUAGE

One of the most important changes in the lives of the population of the Staffordshire Moorlands would have occured in language.

All earlier Celtic and Roman words were more or less obliterated, except for written Latin which returned later with conversion to Christianity.

It is important to remember that Anglo-Saxon formed the very heart, the basis of the language we now speak today. It is an amazing fact that we now have more North American Red Indian words in the English Language than we have Celtic. So ruthless were these new people in imposing their language and culture. They actually called the Romano/British they found here, *'WEALAS' (WELSH)* which means 'foreigners'.

The English Language never has 'taken any prisoners'. It is a 'black-hole' language. It absorbs words from outside and completely changes the spelling, pronunciation and eventually the very meaning. This process still continues today. Countries such as France have actually passed laws to prevent the 'Anglicisation' of their language.

Below is an example of how our Anglo-Saxon Leek ancestors spoke. The form of the language has developed over the centuries, but we still use many of the words today.

The words "The dragon shall dwell in a low, the wolf dwell in the wood, the boar in the thicket, the hawk on the glove, good must strive with evil, light with darkness.

would be spoken and written as follows,

"Draca sceal on hlaewe, wulf sceal on bearow, eofor sceal on holte, hafue sceal on glofe, god sceal wio yfele, leoht sceal wid pystrum".

MYTHICAL BEASTS – REVERSE OF QUEEN'S THRONE VIKING CHESSPIECE.
© 1995 SAXON VILLAGE PROJECT

Another example is,

'But the monster mauling was dark death shadow, old and young he lurked and ambushed in endless night ruled misty moors, men do not know where hell-demons in motion glide'

this would be spoken and written,

'Ac se aeglaeca ehtende waes deorc deapscua du gupe ond geogope seomade ond syrede sinnihte heold mistige moras men ne hwyder hefrunan hwyritum scribas'.

Some more words used by the Leek Anglo-Saxons

Beorht Cristalla	-	Beautiful Crystal
Lybbestre	-	Enchantress
Gimstan	-	Gemstone
Galdorword	-	A magic word
Generstede	-	Sanctuary
Scirham	-	(shining) Armour
Tungalcraeft	-	Astronomy
Gelician	-	Pleasing
Beorht	-	Beautiful
Gemeltan	-	Molten (silver)
Sinchroden	-	Bejewelled
Halig	-	Blessed
Bletsung	-	Blessing
Galdor	-	Charm
Hringedstefna	-	Curved-prowed sailing ship
Mereswin	-	Dolphin
Fandian	-	Explore
Lang Faru	-	Long journey
Beebian	-	Sail on the ebb-tide
Forlidennes	-	Shipwreck
Sumorlida	-	Summer expedition
Paeclando	-	The Peak District
Bachord	-	(book hoard) Library
Blaechorn	-	(Black horn) Inkwell
Windeltreow	-	Willow tree
Brember	-	A bramble
Fifalde	-	A butterfly
Wudufaesten	-	A camp protected by trees
Mistilitan	-	Mistletoe
Rudubeam	-	A red tree
Ruduberge	-	A red berry
Windelstan	-	A round tower
Corenbeg	-	A crown
Werod	-	Bodyguard
Adelborennes	-	A noble
Aedelu	-	A noble family

The second extract is from an Anglo-Saxon poem called, **Beowulf'.**
It is 3,000 lines long and was written in the language of the Anglo-Saxons. It is believed to have evolved in the Kingdom of Mercia at the time of King Offa 757 - 796 AD.

Below are just a few of the many Anglo-Saxon words;

AECERN ....acorn   FORHTIAN ......afraid
LYFT ..... air   ENGEL ....angel
CRAEFT ...art    BACAN ....bake
BEER ....beer   ASCIAN ....ask
WECCAN ...awake   BERN .....barn
GETIMBRE ...building   CUMAN ....come
HUNIG ....honey   RINAN ...rain
SPRECAN ...speak   STANWEALL ..stone wall
SWEORD ... sword   WINCIAN ...wink

THE FIRST SAXON SETTLEMENT IN LEEK

The Saxon settlers would have been attracted to the Leek area by the fertile soil of the valleys and lowlands, as well as the sheep grazing areas in the moorlands. We know from much archaeolgical evidence and documentation that the Saxons settled in this area. Part of this evidence comes in the form of place-names which abound. Names such as, **'Bradnop, Tittesworth, Rudyard, Onecote, Grindon, Butterton,** and finally of course, **' LEEK ',** itself.

Saxons settlers always 'homed- in' on areas that had already been well developed agriculturally. Leek was just such a place, and it would have perfectly suited the needs of the Saxon farmers.

For some reason the Anglo-Saxons tended not to locate their settlements alongside exisiting roads. Perhaps they felt this made them more vunerable to attack. They preferred to live away from the road. This explains the positioning of some Saxon

49

settlements in the Staffordshire Moorlands. For example, 'Meerbrook" is about a mile away from the line of the Leek to Buxton Roman Road - And the original central area of Saxon Leek is situated close to the site of St. Edward's Church.

RELIGION AND MAGIC

When the Saxons first arrived in England they were Pagans, while the native Romano/British were still Christian. In time all of England became Pagan. When Christiantiy returned it merely 'blended-in' with the old pagan religion.

It has been noted by some historians that England during this time would not have been a place for the 'faint hearted', as the few Chrisitian missionaries from Europe attempted to convert the Pagan Lords to Christianity. Many Lords did convert and they took their people with them. However, the idea that they abandoned their old religion is wishful thinking. One Saxon Lord merely put up two shrines at different ends of his Hall. One was dedicated to the Christian God, the other to the Pagan God! Burial sites from this time also often contained both Christian and Pagan relics

In order to understand the religious beliefs of the first Saxon pagan settlers of Leek, we have to go back in time to the year 98 AD. This was the time of the most famous, Cornelius Tacitus. This ancient Roman wrote an account of life in Britain and also a fasinating book called, **'GERMANIA'.**

Tacitus recounts some amusing details of the Romano/British, like the fact that our ancestors were 'very partial to geese' and that 'collective marriages' were very popular. However, it is his descriptions of the religious practices of the Saxon Germanic people, who were later to settle in Leek and the Staffordshire Moorlands which are of most interest here.

For example, we are told that the Saxon Germanic people believed that both holiness and the gift of prophecy resided in women. Tacitus also praises these people for their great morality. Sanctity of marriage was one of the mainstays of the society. This great respect for women was carried over into their Pagan Religion.

We know from Tacitus that the people who lived in Jutland worshipped the goddess, Nerthus or Mother Earth. Tacitus wrote,

"THERE IS ON AN ISLAND IN THE OCEAN AN INVIOLATE GROVE, AND IN IT A CONSECRATED CAR (CHARIOT) COVERED WITH A ROBE; ONLY ONE PRIEST IS ALLOWED TO TOUCH IT. HE PERCEIVES WHEN THE GODDESS IS THERE IN THE SANCTUARY, AND HE ACCOMPANIES HER WITH GREAT REVERENCE AS SHE IS DRAWN ALONG BY HEIFERS. THEN THERE ARE DAYS OF REJOICING, AND FESTIVE IS THE PLACE WHICH SHE HONOURS. MEN DO NOT GO INTO BATTLE, NOR CARRY ARMS, ONLY PEACE IS KNOWN...THE DIVINITY IS WASHED IN A SECRET LAKE. SLAVES PERFORM THIS, THEY ARE IMMEDIATELY SWALLOWED UP BY THE SAME LAKE....HENCE ARISES A MYSTERIOUS TERROR'.

This is a strange description indeed, and we are left to wonder just what was the 'mysterious terror'!

We are also told that, in other parts of the continent the male Pagan Priests dressed like women.

All this is just a brief example of the kind of religious beliefs held by our first Leek Saxon ancestors.

The burial place of a pagan Saxon Priestess was excavated in Kent (England). In the grave were found gold brocaded fillets, as well as perforated spoons and crystal spheres - all these were located alongside the body. A pagan Saxon Priest was not allowed to ride on anything but a mare, and it was believed he could defeat an enemy simply by standing on a mound or 'low' and chanting a spell.

Written charms, folk-lore and excavations can give us some idea of the pagan religious practices at that time. We know the English Saxons believed in *'ERCE - THE MOTHER OF THE EARTH'*. Another goddess, *'EOSTRE'*, was the Goddess of Spring. If this sounds familiar, it is because it gave us the word, 'Easter' - one example of the 'blending' of the old Saxon/Pagan and new Christian religions.

Animals also figured greatly. The symbol of the Boar was thought to have magical protective powers, and an emblem of a boar was placed on the helmets of Lords and Kings. The gods, Woden, Thunor and Tiw were also worshipped by our Saxon ancestors.

In the 'NINE HERB CHARMS' we read,

'......... THE SNAKE CAME CREEPING. IT TORE A MAN TO PIECES. THEN TOOK WODEN NINE GLORIOUS TWIGS AND STRUCK THE ADDER SO THAT IT FLEW INTO NINE PARTS.'

RUNESTONE MONUMENT WITH SERPENT. RUNES PAINTED INSIDE THE SNAKE'S BODY. © 1995 SAXON VILLAGE PROJECT

The Leek Anglo Saxons were farmers so it was important the land stayed fertile. In fact land, crops and animals were the main-stay of Anglo-Saxon society.

For this reason charms and prayers were recited to, 'help the land'. These Germanic charms and spells were used to ward off natural disorder, witchcraft, evil and ill-health.

One pagan charm called, '*THE UNFRUITFUL LAND*', instructed people to put oil, honey, milk and holy-water on the land. Four turfs then had to be taken from the corners of the ground - these were then carried to a holy pagan site, or in later times to a Christian church (site of St. Edward's Church) where chants were said over them. The turfs were then returned to the land and a shaft or cross of Quickbeam was raised on the earth. The words of the charm spoke of the, 'Sun God' and 'Mother Earth'.

When Christianity arrived many of the Germanic pagan feasts, festivals and rituals remained more or less intact - in fact we still use them today - only the names of the gods were changed - The effect on the everyday religious practices of the Saxons would have been minimal.

'*ELF-SHOT*' was the word used for rheumatism, because it was thought elves shot tiny arrows into people which caused pain. Saxon women burnt handfuls of grain to promote health in the household, and girls sat on the top of warm bread ovens to drive out fever.

Our Anglo-Saxon Leek ancestors were very skilled in the use of herbs as medicines. Illness was seen as an evil, and they believed chants and prayers gave these herbs extra strength to do their work. The '*NINE HERB CHARMS*' was used to protect against illness and evil. Part of it reads,

'*UNA PU HATTEST YLDOST WYRTA, DU MIHT WID 3 AND WID 30 PU MIHT WIP ATTRE, AND WID ONFLYGE. NU MAGON PAS NINE WYRTA WID NYGON WULDORGEFLOGENUM*'.

which translated means

Thou wert called una, the oldest of herbs, thou power against 3 and against 30, thou power against poison and infection. Now these 9 herbs have power against 9 evil spirits.'

ANGLO SAXON INTERTWINED DRAGONS
© 1995 SAXON VILLAGE PROJECT

52

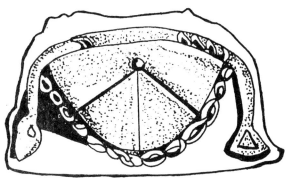

A SAXON STONE SUNDIAL OF THE EARLY 8TH CENTURY THE THREE 'TIME' LINES CORRESPOND TO DAYLIGHT HOURS OF PRAYER, 'TERCE', 'SEXT' AND 'NONE'. SUNDIALS LIKE THIS WOULD HAVE BEEN COMMONPLACE ON SAXON CHURCHES. NOTE THE SERPENT AND THE SAXON KNOT DESIGN.

Ann Biddulph '98

SUN, MOON AND SEASONS - The Anglo-Saxon calendar was different to today's. They did not have clocks for accurate time keeping, so the year was divided-up according to the movement of the planets, the phases of the moon and the relationship between the time of year and the work that had to be done on the land.

The year was only divided into two seasons, *'WINTRUS' - 'THE TIME WHEN THE WEATHER IS WET',* and *'SUMOR' - SUMMER OR 'HALF-YEAR'.*

There were 12 parts to the calendar. For example,

The first 'TIME' of the year was, *'AEFTERA GEOLA' - 'THE TIME AFTER YULE - THE TIME FOR PLOUGHING'.*

The 6th. 'TIME' of the year was, *AERRA LIPA' - 'WOOD CUTTING TIME'.*

The 7th. 'TIME' was, *'WEODMONAP' - 'THE WEED MONTH - THE TIME FOR REAPING'*

The 10th 'TIME' was *'WINTER FYLLEPMONAP' - 'THE TIME OF THE FIRST FULL MOON OF WINTER - THE TIME FOR FALCON HUNTING.*

'LECTEN' was *'THE TIME WHEN THE DAYS BECOME LONGER'.* This was not a religious time, but merely an observation of the number of hours of daylight. Today we call that time, *'LENT'.* Again, *'HAERFEST'* was not referring to a season, but to a specific agricultural time when the harvest could be safely brought in.

GODS OF THE HARVEST

© COPYRIGHT 1995 SAXON VILLAGE PROJECT

We know of mythical 'harvest figures' or 'gods' from Saxon times. *'SHEAF'* was one and his son *'BEOW' - BARLEY.* From these developed the custom of making 'Corn Dolls'. These 'dolls' would be kept by the Leek farmers until the following spring to 'carry over' the fertility of the land for the next ploughing and sowing.

SAXON DAYS OF THE WEEK

MONANDAEG - DAY OF THE MOON

TIWESDAEG - DAY OF GOD TIW

WODENESDAEG - DAY OF THE GOD WODEN

THUNRESDAEG - DAY OF THOR GOD OF THE SKY

FRIGESDAEG - DAY OF THE GODDESS FRIG

SAETERNEDDAEG - DAY OF SATURN

SUNNANDAEG - THE SUN'S DAY. - The idea of the seventh day being a holy or rest day was not understood by the early Anglo-Saxons

A Feast was held in the 2nd month of the year in which cakes were offered to the gods.

At the Autumn feast came the slaughtering of cattle. This gave November its name, that of 'SACRIFICE MONTH'. At this time all the left-over bones were gathered together and burnt on a great fire. These were known as 'BONE-FIRES'.

WE STILL CARRY OUT THIS SAXON CEREMONY TODAY ON 'BONFIRE NIGHT'!

This is just one of the many Saxon ceremonies that people, sometimes unknowingly, still 'celebrate' today.

TWO DRAGONS INTERTWINED ON NOSE GUARD
OF ANGLOSAXON HELMET 8TH CENT.

© 1995 SAON VILLAGE PROJECT

DRAGONS, DEMONS AND DWARFS

The definite 'belief' that DRAGONS lived in burial mounds is evident in Anglo-Saxon folk-lore and poetry.

Beowulf, an Anglo-Saxon fictional hero, slayed a fiery dragon which had attacked him when he visited a burial mound. In the poem 'Beowulf', it tells us how the Dragon guarded the treasure in the 'low'.

The treasure came from Mother Earth. It says,

54

'THEN THE MIGHTY TREASURE, THE GOLD OF ANCIENTS WAS WRAPPED UP IN SPELLS (ENCHANTMENT) SO THAT IT MAY NOT BE TOUCHED BY MAN UNTIL GOD HIMSELF GAVE PERMISSION FOR MAN TO OPEN THE HOARD'.

To steal a dragon's treasure would have brought a curse down on the thief.

The Dragon was called a *'WYRM'* - *'DRACA'*. This was thought to be a 'coiled', scaley monster that could fly. It had fiery breath and a poisonous bite. It only attacked men who came to steal its treasure.

A Demon called a, *SCUCCA'* was also thought to live in burial mounds.

These stories may well have been used as a deliberate ploy to keep the curious and the robber away, as mentioned in a previous chapter that refers to, 'The Green Dragon' of Leek.

Other creatures from this time were *'YLFE'* - *'ELVES'*. These were not the little woodland beings we know today, but very evil things which brought disease and nightmares.

There were also, *'DIVEORG'* - *'DWARFS'* . Darkness was supposed to hide supernatural beings that resembled wolves and ravens. This was the start of Man's belief in 'Werewolves'. The Saxon word for 'Man' was *'WER'*. The word for 'Wolf' was *'WULF'*. Today 'Werewolf' or 'Werwolf' still means a 'Wolfman'.

THE SAXON CROSSES OF LEEK

The Anglo-Saxons were great ones for carved stone crosses and one unique feature of Saxon England was the raising of these stones. They were erected to indicate special holy sites - later they became known as 'Churchways' as they often marked the entrance to a Saxon Christian church.

In the church of St. Edward's in Leek, there are four examples of these Saxon crosses.

One consists of a rectangular cross shaft. It has a carved panel of plait work. It is thought to date from the 9th. Century.

The second is a round shafted type, about eleven feet high.

There are also two fragments of a wheel-head cross. These are located in the organ transept, and most likely found there way there when the church was being rebuilt in later centuries.

55

TWO OF THE ANGLO SAXON STONE CROSSES IN ST. EDWARD'S CHURCHYARD

THE CALVARY STONE - The most outstanding example is The Calvary Stone which was found when part of the church wall collapsed in 1896.

This stone forms part of a rectangular shafted cross. The sides have interlaced ornamentation and carved figure which is said to depict Christ carrying the Cross. The spaces on each side of the main figure are filled with a serpent-like creature.

The stone was cut from local gritstone and is but a small section of much taller shaft that once stood proudly on the site. Sadly and amazingly, it was used as a building stone for the churchyard wall in 1751. It seems some of our 18th. century ancestors had little appreciation of Leek's Saxon heritage.

There are a number of other Saxon crosses in the surrounding villages in the Moorlands, for example Ilam and Alstonfield.

(The Calvary stone is referred to again in the later Viking chapter)

THE MERCIAN BEAST - THIS WAS A DRAGON LIKE CREATURE WHICH WAS SPECIAL TO ANGLOSAXON ART AND STONE CARVING IN MERCIA. THE BEST REMAINING EXAMPLE OF THIS CAN BE FOUND IN DERBYSHIRE.

PAGAN TO CHRISTIAN

When the Christian Saxons put up their stone crosses in Leek they were acting in accordance with instructions from Pope Gregory in Rome who told everyone that they had to turn earlier Pagan temples into Christian churches or meeting places.

Any temple that existed at the present site of St. Edward's would have been removed and the Saxon Crosses and a simple church erected in its place.

In 627, Coife who was the High Pagan Priest to King Edwin, heard about the new Christian God. We are told that,

'Girded with a sword and spear in his hand he mounted the King's stallion and rode up to the Pagan idols.. As soon as he reached the temple, he cast his spear into it and profaned it'

The Anglo-Saxons were to record, in Latin, many similar events at that time.

56

MYTHICAL BEAST STONE CARVING FROM A STONE CROSS SHAFT. A BLEND OF ANGLOSAXON & VIKING 10TH CENT. DERBYSHIRE.
© *1995 SAXON VILAGE PROJECT*

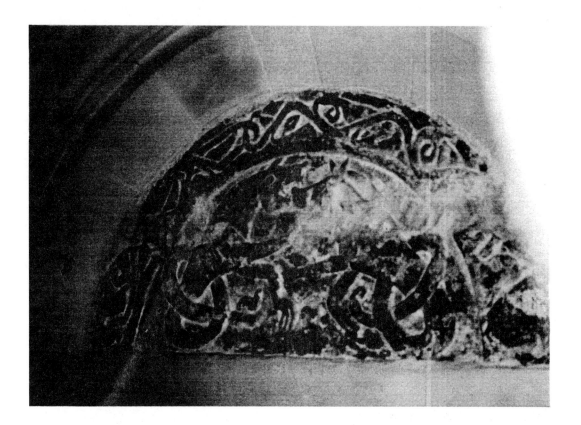

The above photograph shows the Anglo Saxon Tympanum set inside the church in the village of Ipstones. It depicts two fighting, mythical beasts with intertwined tails. This Tympanum is all that is left of an earlier Saxon church which was replaced in later times. We know that a small chapel existed there during the time of Dieulacres Abbey when Ipstones was part of the Parish of Leek.

Ipstones is an AngloSaxon place name — and like many other such villages in the Staffordshire Moorlands, it has a rich history stretching far back in time

SAXON BUILDINGS

The first Saxons to arrive here built their houses of timber and plaster, even though there were still Romano British stone masons living amongst them. Many of these stone masons were forced to move to the continent in order to find work.

The Saxons, when they later built in stone, were influenced by the classical Roman style of building, and this was used in buildings such as churches and halls. The arches were light and rounded, and the windows were very pointed at the top.

We have a description from a Saxon in Ramsy, called Byrhtferth, on the building of houses. He wrote,

'FIRST ONE EXAMINES THE SITE, AND ALSO HEWS THE TIMBER AND FITS FAIRLY THE SILL, THEN HE LAYS DOWN THE BEAMS AND FASTENS THE RAFTERS TO THE RIDGE-POLE AND SUPPORTS IT WITH STRONG BUTTRESSES AND AFTERWARDS HE ADORNS THE HOUSE PLEASANTLY'.

Some Saxon houses were not always too reliable. There is a recorded incident when a number of Saxon Christian bishops were killed after the floor of the upstairs chamber in a hall where they were staying collapsed.

The saw had not yet been invented, so felled trees were split along their grain using axes. This meant that the beams and uprights of the houses were not straight, but they could be extremely strong and long lasting. Modern methods of carpentry today cut right through the grain. This weakens the wood and causes warping. If you want to see an example of this ancient method of building, then visit the 18th. Century James Brindley Water Mill in Leek. Here the wood in the roof beams has been split along the natural grain in the 'Anglo-Saxon' way.

The larger Saxon halls had trestle tables and fixed wooden benches. There would be mattresses and pillows on the floor, and the walls would be hung with rich tapestries.

The everyday houses were plain, thatched wooden buildings. The floor was hollowed out, then wooden oak beams were placed across to form a strong floor. Large oak posts held up the roof. The roof was decoratively thatched with reeds, much the same as thatched houses are today. Fish, meat and herbs were hung along the beams We know that many of the Saxon halls were extremely high, large and imposing. The insides were quite magnificent with their huge, soaring roof beams and great fireplaces.

As mentioned previously, when the English Saxons became Christianised they began to build their houses and churches in stone. They would often re-use the stone from any previous Roman buildings. In fact, the Anglo-Saxons were greatly impressed with the Roman buildings, the paved roads and the giant ramparts which enclosed Roman forts.

In the 'Anglo-Saxon Chronicles' they call the Roman buildings,

'THE WORKS OF GIANTS... CITIES ARE CONSPICUOUS FROM AFAR, THE CUNNING WORK OF GIANTS, - 'CAESTRA BEOD FEORRAN GESYNE, ORDANC ENTA GEWEORC'.

An Anglo-Saxon poet also wrote at that time,

'THUS THE CREATOR OF MEN LAID WASTE THIS HABITATION, THE OLD WORKS OF GIANTS STOOD DESOLATE.' He goes on to describe the men who lived there as,

'MEN BRIGHT WITH GOLD, ADORNED RESPLENDENTLY, PROUD AND FLUSHED WITH WINE, THEY SHONE IN THEIR WAR-GEAR, THEY GAZED ON TREASURE, ON SILVER, ON GEMS, ON RICHES, ON THE BRIGHT CITIDEL OF A SPACIOUS KINGDOM'.

Little wonder then that the remains of Roman Fort situated at 'Wall-Grange', Leek, was later referred to by the Medieval monks from Dieulacrest Abbey as 'a Castle'.

MEASUREMENT AND COINAGE

The Saxons had their own ways of measurement.

A ROD WAS 15 GERMANIC FEET.

THE WORDS 'ACRE' AND 'FURLONG' ARE SAXON. AN 'AECER' MEANT A WHOLE FIELD.

A 'FURLONG' WAS A LONG FURROW.

These words are still with us today. Unfortunately the English people are being forced to give up their heritage. There are a great many scholars and historians who believe that these measurements have become so much a part of our cultural heritage that is is wrong they are not being preserved. Not only should they be taught to our children in school, but they should not be replaced by a metric system. Can you imagine what the French would do if they were forced to give up an important part of their heritage? There would be rioting in the streets of Paris! Why should the English always be the ones having to make the sacrifice?

58

One scholar of Anglo-Saxon was recently quoted as saying, "the modern metrication is a subjugation of the English people by bureaucracy using threat and deception.' It is true that English trades-people and those in business can now face criminal charges if they fail to use the metric system. The irony is, shop keepers in France are legally allowed to sell goods weighed and measured in English feet, pounds, etc.

KING ALFRED MUST BE TURNING IN HIS GRAVE!!

COINAGE

The Leek Saxons, like the rest of Mercia, used currency called

THE 'SESTER', THE 'AMBER' AND THE 'MANCUS' WHICH WAS 70 GRAINS OF GOLD OR THIRTY SILVER PIECES. THE 'MARK' WAS A SILVER 20 PENCE. THE 'SHILLING' WAS VALUED AT 20 PENCE IN KENT, BUT ONLY 4 PENCE IN MERCIA.

SILVER ANGLO SAXON PENNIES
© 1995 SAXON VILLAGE PROJECT

SAXON WOMEN

As mentioned before, women held a special place in Anglo-Saxon society. They were known as , *'FREODUWEBBE' OR THE 'WEAVERS OF PEACE'.*

They were thought to hold the power of prophesy. During the wedding ceremony the man and woman laid their hands on a sword. This recognised the husband's strength and powers of protection, and the wife's role as peacemaker.

Women often travelled between villages to marry, and royal ladies even travelled to other kingdoms. Marriage was sometimes used as a way of uniting land owning families.

Anglo-Saxon graves which have been excavated have brought to light women's jewellery and decorative shells which actually originated in Egypt.

Most jewellery was worn by women. Square headed and circular brooches were used for pinning cloaks.

Anglo-Saxon jewellery was some of the finest ever produced in Europe, its beauty and intricate workmanship today has to be seen to be believed.

Anglo Saxon Dress
ᚠᛏᚷᚴᛖ ᚠᚠᚴᛏ ᚱᛗᚻᚻ

© Saxon Village Project 1995

Even as early as the 8th century,
Anglo Saxon ladies paid much attention
to fashion.
Anglo Saxon England was
famous throughout Christendom for
its unique embroidery & tapestry
work, and the wives and daughters of
noblemen wore beautifully embroidered
dresses & cloaks, along with undergarments
made from Scandinavian silk. Their shoes were
fashioned from soft leather, dyed bright red. Like their men folk, women
too crimped their hair, but they also wore long veils held up with ribbons.
Their jewellery was crafted more finely from silver and gold and often
studded with precious stones. It was the fashion for ladies to grow their
nails and then to file them carefully until they resembled eagle's talons.
Although lower class women would have worn plain, woollen clothes for
work, on feast days and at times of celebration they bedecked themselves
in colourful, embroidered garments and wore simple jewellery with
decorative ribbons & veils. The costumes of the wealthy Anglo Saxons
became very elaborate as time went on, and women's skirts especially
became extremely long and flowing.
The above illustration, taken from an actual Anglo Saxon drawing, shows
a Saxon girl dancing at a feast – note the soft delicate flow of the elaborate
dress that clearly reveals the line of the body under the fine material.
Dancers, musicians, poets and storytellers travelled from hall to hall, such
as the Saxon Lord of the Manor's hall built on the present site of the
Market Place in Leek. In return these entertainers were given a meal, gold,
silver rings and a place to sleep for the night.

The richer Saxon women wore undergarments of red or blue silk ; the head dresses and sleeves of their gowns were also made from this material. Shoes were adorned with red dyed animal skin. Both men and women had the hair on their temples and foreheads crimped with curlers. Women's hair was covered with a fine veil, held up with ribbon, which then hung down as far as the feet. The lower classes made do with simpler, dyed woollen garments.

It was the Saxon fashion to sharpen the fingernails until, 'they looked like hawks talons'.

The most finely and richly dressed were the King, his Lords and Warriors.

ROADS AND TRAVEL

The Anglo-Saxons inherited a network of tracks and roads from previous times, much of which we still use today.

There was rapid contact between the Anglo-Saxon communities in England, although most of the ordinary people stayed within their own kingdom. Slaves were not allowed to move freely.

Traders brought salt from Cheshire and lead from Derbyshire. Iron was traded all over the country to make ploughshares, fish-hooks, spears, helmets and weapons.

Christian Pilgrims travelled to holy shrines. Invalids were transported by carts to places of healing - And it was expected that all travellers be given hospitality and charity in the towns and villages they passed through.

All travellers depended on a sure supply of water, and water was carried about in skin-bags by 'WETMAUNGRES' OR 'WATER-SELLERS'. In later Christian times pure sources of water were blessed by the priests. This water would then be sold as 'holy water' - And while they were about it, the priests also sold relics of saints which were supposed to guard against evil.

THE SAXON LAW

Under Anglo-Saxon law, disputes had to be settled by arbitration. The views on moral right and wrong were somewhat different from today.

Most of the disputes were about land or animals. If a Freeman stole from another he had to pay back three times what he had stolen.

Each part of the human body had a value. A simple bruise was worth five shillings. If a thief broke into a house, the householder had the legal right to kill him, as long as it was before sunrise. If the thief broke into the house after sunrise, the householder could claim he had killed the thief in self-defence.

KING ALFRED BASED HIS LAW ON THE BIBLE AND THE TEN COMMANDMENTS.

He said it was very wrong for anyone to harm children or widows. The King had the absolute right to slay any person who harmed a child using his own royal sword. No one was allowed to harm or cut down a tree unless it was on his own land.

POETRY AND MUSIC

Harp players and singers travelled all around the countryside. They were paid by villagers and Lords to sing and perform. A poem of the time says,

'*RAED SCEAL MON SECGAN, RUNE WRITEN, LEOP GESINGAN, LOFES GAERNIAN*'

WHICH MEANS

'*A MAN SHALL UTTER WISDOM, WRITE RUNES, SING SONGS, EARN PRAISE*'.

Families and Kinsmen gathered together around the fire in houses and halls to sing songs, tell ancient tales and recite poetry, such as 'Beowulf'.

These tales and poems were not at first written down, but were remembered by the '*the story-tellers*' who would pass their knowledge on down through their children.

Some of these poems and stories were extremely long, and required a great amount of learning.

People also played dice and chess. There was stag, boar and fox-hunting, horse racing and hawking for the Saxon Royals and Nobles.

LOCAL SAXON FINDS

THE BENTY GRANGE ROYAL BURIAL - The most famous and richest Anglo-Saxon site was excavated by Thomas Bateman at Benty Grange Farm, south west of Buxton. Although it is not strictly speaking within our own immediate geographical area, it is such an important find that it warrants special mention.

The site is the burial place of a 7th. century Anglo-Saxon Prince Warrior from the Pecsaetan Saxons. The most amazing artefact discovered there was the Anglo-Saxon Helmet. It was made up of iron bands and attached to these was a small cross of silver. These bands held horn plates. The helmet was decorated with a Boar Crest. The animal had eyes of garnets set in gold and was decorated with silver studs and Roman plates of cut silver.

The Boar was a sacred symbol and was connected to the Pagan God Freyer. The helmet was most likely made at the time when Christiantiy was being introduced into this area. It is an example of how Pagan and Christian religious symbols were often used together, as they still are today - We use the Christian cross at Eastertime along with the Easter Egg which is an old pagan symbol of Spring.

The remains of a leather drinking cup decorated with silver crosses was also found on the site as well as three escutcheons. These were decorated with three serpents. These finds can now be seen at Sheffield City Museum and the Ashmolean Museum in Oxford. No weapons or body were found there - It is thought that the barrow had already been robbed at some time in its history.

THE PRINCES HELMET, CUP &
FINDS FROM BENTY GRANGE-
THOMAS BATEMAN.

TO THE SAXON SETTLERS WHO CAME HERE, THE LEEK MOORLANDS WAS A 'NEW ENGLAND'. THEIR STORY WHICH BEGAN IN EUROPE CENTURIES BEFORE IS OUR STORY. THEY CARVED OUT A NEW BEGINNING IN A LAND ABANDONED BY THE ROMANS. THEIR NEXT TASK WAS TO FACE, OVERCOME AND EVENTUALLY ABSORB THE SCANDANAVIAN VIKING INVADERS.

Anglo Saxon Dress
ᚠᛏᚷᛚᚠ ᛋᚠᛁᚠᛏ ᚻᛗᛋᛋ

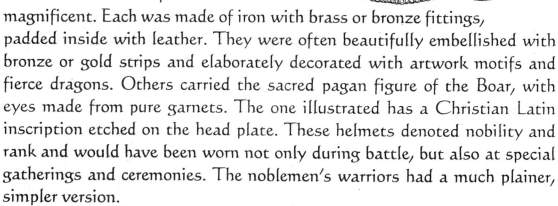

The illustration on the right shows the type of helmet worn by the AngloSaxon noblemen who ruled over Mercia & the Staffordshire Moorlands during the 700's AD, before the coming of the Vikings. It is very similar to the helmet found in the royal Saxon burial low at Benty Grange, nr. Hartington.
These helmets were quite magnificent. Each was made of iron with brass or bronze fittings, padded inside with leather. They were often beautifully embellished with bronze or gold strips and elaborately decorated with artwork motifs and fierce dragons. Others carried the sacred pagan figure of the Boar, with eyes made from pure garnets. The one illustrated has a Christian Latin inscription etched on the head plate. These helmets denoted nobility and rank and would have been worn not only during battle, but also at special gatherings and ceremonies. The noblemen's warriors had a much plainer, simpler version.

Some people still fail to appreciate that the Anglo Saxons were an extremely civilised and cultured people. When not in military dress, the noblemen wore brightly coloured, attractively embroidered clothes made from finely woven wool and silk, along with exquisitely made gold and silver jewellery often set with precious stones. Their faces were clean-shaven except for a carefully groomed, long moustache. The hair was cut and crimped into waves, which framed the face. Historical records show that good manners and chivalry were all important.

ᚻᚠᚾ ᛏᚻᛗ ᚱᚠᚷᚠᛏ ᚲᚱᚠᛏᛗᛚᛏ ᛏᚻᚾᛋᛗ ᚹᚾᚠ ᚱᛗᚠᚻ ᛏᚻᛁᛋ ᛒᚠᚠᚢ

THE VIKING INFLUENCE IN SAXON TIMES
AND THE NAMING OF LEEK

The Anglo-Saxon Chronicles tell us some interesting facts about the coming of the Vikings. For example it records that in 789 AD.

'THERE CAME FOR THE FIRST TIME 3 SHIPS OF NORTHMEN. THOSE WERE THE FIRST SHIPS OF DANISH MEN WHICH CAME TO THE LAND OF THE ENGLISH'.

It also states that in 991 AD after the great Battle of Maldon when the Saxons fought against further invasions that,

'IN THAT YEAR IT WAS DECIDED FOR THE FIRST TIME TO PAY TRIBUTE TO THE DANES BECAUSE OF THE GREAT TERROR THEY INSPIRED ALONG THE COAST...THE DANEGELD WAS TEN THOUSAND POUNDS'.

The paying of the Danegeld, which was revenue raised by the Saxons to 'buy-off' the Danish invaders, only encouraged the enemy to expect more. After many battles England became an Anglo-Danish kingdom under an 'EALDERMAN' or nobleman appointed by the King.

By 1016 AD England was part of a great Scandanavian Empire and the people of the Staffordshire Moorlands were living under the 'DANELAW' system of government.

The well constructed roads, a legacy of previous Roman rule, were still in use. This helped in the movement of the new armies. The Vikings also brought many horses with them, which allowed them to travel easily and quickly over rough terrain.

It is important to stress the fact that these new invaders did not pose a threat to the Saxon English in the way the Romans had to the early Britons and the Germanic Saxons had to the Romano British.

The reason for this is that the English Saxons and the Vikings both originated from northern Europe. Not only did they look the same, but they also shared the same culture.

63

MORE IMPORTANTLY, THE LANGUAGE OF THE SAXONS AND THE VIKINGS WERE COUSIN LANGUAGES. All these were very significant factors at a time when the ordinary people rarely left the individual kingdoms, such as Mercia, in which they resided.

THE ARRIVAL OF THE VIKINGS IN THE LEEK MOORLANDS

As the migrating Viking warriors moved across the country, they settled down as farmers and traders. In time they were to take over the Kingdom of Mercia, of which Leek was part.

We know that the Vikings came up towards LEEK from the East, along the valley of the River Trent. We can pick out the place-names which tell us of their presence. The place-name, 'WENSLEY' means 'Woden's Ley'. - 'LEY' is a Saxon word meaning, 'a clearing in a wood'. 'WEN' was actually spelt as 'WODEN' in its earliest form.

This tells us that the present day 'WENSLEY' is located on the site of a wood which contained a pagan shrine to the Viking god WODEN

Fifteen miles from Leek lies, 'FRIDEN' nr. Hartington. This ancient place-name actually means 'Frya's Valley', - 'DEN' being the Saxon word for 'valley'. FRYA was the Viking Goddess of Fertility, and again the place-name tells us that a shrine to the Goddess Frya was sited at that particular place.

The Viking settlers who eventually reached Leek and the Leek Moorlands would have found the area under the powerful domination of the Anglo-Saxon Lords.

The lower, fertile areas still formed part of the large Saxon estates. The Norse men who came to here would have been granted marginal or secondary land to farm on. It would have been more of a 'drift' than an invasion, and the Leek Saxons and Vikings lived easily alongside each other.

In time, as the Viking settlement and influence grew in this area, these Saxon estates or 'WAPENTAKES' were taken over or given as gifts to the Viking leaders. In fact there was much buying and selling of land between the Saxons and Vikings at that time.

'THORP' nr. Ilam was a Scandanavian settlement and was most likely to have been a secondary settlement to a much larger farming estate. 'THORP' which is a Viking word for 'hamlet is found widely today in both Sweden and Denmark.

Two other places, 'UPPER HULME' and 'HULME END' give evidence of a Scandanavian origin.

The Vikings set up their own farmsteads or 'SAETRS' for sheep and arable farming.   They were an extrovert, unconventional people who greatly reinforced the English Saxon culture which existed. They were also avid traders and would have breathed new life into Leek, which was already an important trading centre. The Saxon Kings of Mercia had promoted growth of towns such as Leek, but under the Vikings this growth would have been sudden and dramatic. The Viking merchant became a familiar figure wherever buying and selling was taking place. They traded in exotic goods such as, imported amber, walrus ivory, continental purple silk and rich spices from the Far East. To carry their goods between towns such as Leek and Derby they used wickerwork carts drawn by horses or oxen. Heavy waggons, re-inforced with leather, were used for longer distances. Because the Vikings were a sea-faring people they used boats and 'long-ships' whenever they could. The English Saxons too were fine sailors and they built beautiful 'long- ships' powered by as many as 20 oarsmen.

THE SIMILARITY OF LANGUAGE

As mentioned earlier, the main factor that helped to foster peaceful co-existence was the similarity of language. The Saxon and Viking languages were Cousin languages. Many of the words were the same, they differed only in the pronunciation.

One classic example of this concerns a garment worn at that time. This was a long woollen tunic which reached down to the knees and was fastened with a belt around the middle. The Saxon English called this a 'SHIRT' (soft pronunciation).
The Viking settlers called it a 'SKIRT' (hard pronunciation).
Although both names referred exactly to the same thing, as time went on a 'shirt' began to apply to the upper part of the garment, the 'skirt' to the lower.

We now use these same two words today.

A similar thing occured with the words 'SHIP' and 'SKIP'.
'SHIP' (soft) was the Saxon pronunication for a boat. 'SKIP' (hard) was the Viking

pronunciation. Again we still use the words, 'ship' and 'skip' And a 'SKIPPER' is a term used for the Captain of a boat.

If we could travel back in time and say to a Leek Saxon/Viking woman, "Mak me sum fodder", she would know exactly what you meant, "Make me some food". In fact some Leek people still talk this way now!!

For the Saxons a 'WINDOW' was a hole or an eye in a building where the wind could come in. The Vikings pronounced it as 'VINDOW'.

Another example closer to home is the word 'CHETIL' (soft pronunciation). It has come down to us today as the word 'KETTLE' (hard). It also survives in the local place name 'CHEDDLETON' nr. Leek. The name 'Cheddleton' (soft pronunciation) means 'A HOLLOW OR KETTLE SHAPED VALLEY'.

Another example of this is 'KETTLESHULME'. The word 'HULME' is a Danish word 'HULM' and means either a 'water meadow' or 'an island in a wet place'.

Moving on from this we can say with certainty that the actual core, the very heart of the English language today is made up of original Anglo Saxon words, some with Viking pronunciation.

Every word in the following sentence dates from Saxon Times...
"Freezing, heavy snowfalls came to Leek yesterday morning when winter took an early grip on the North Staffordshire Moorlands'!

VIKING BROOCH WITH HORSEMAN
HOLDING SPEAR WITH BOTH HANDS
© COPYRIGHT 1995 SAXON VILLAGE PROJECT

ANCIENT PLACE NAMES IN THE LEEK MOORLANDS

PLACE NAME	MEANING
Leek – *AngloSaxon/Norse*	A (holy) spring or 'leak' from Mother Earth
Bradnop – *AngloSaxon*	A broad blind valley enclosed by moorland
Cheddleton – *AngloSaxon*	A settlement in a deep narrow valley
Cauldon – *AngloSaxon*	Calf-hill
The Churnet – *Old British*	Pre-AngloSaxon river name, meaning unknown
Coombes Brook – *Old Britons & AngloSaxon*	A deep valley
Wall Bridge – *AngloSaxon*	The Fortification or Wall. *The place name 'wall' <u>always</u> refers to Roman activity or to a Roman presence*
Hare-Gate – *Viking*	This means 'soldier's road' and refers exclusively to the near-by Buxton to Leek Roman Road.
Gun Hill – *AngloSaxon*	'Gun' a development of 'dun' Anglo-Saxon for 'hill'
Flash – *Old Danish 'flask'*	A marshy pool
Foxt – *AngloSaxon*	A fox's burrow
Froghall – *Middle English*	The hollow of the frogs
Hulme – *Old Danish*	A dry island in a marshy area
Ipstones – *AngloSaxon*	Ippa's (personal name) stone *or* a raised look-out stone (*'stan' AngloSaxon for 'stone'*)
Leek Frith – *AngloSaxon*	Leek wood (*'frith' = 'wood'*)
Longsdon – *AngloSaxon*	The long hill
Meerbrook – *AngloSaxon*	The boundary brook (*'meer' AngloSaxon for 'boundary'*)
Morridge – *AngloSaxon*	The moorland ridge
The Roaches – *Norman French 'Dieulacres Abbey'*	The Rocks
Hen Cloud – *AngloSaxon*	A high rocky hill
Alton – *AngloSaxon*	Aelfa's (personal name) settlement

Ashcombe – *AngloSaxon*	A narrow valley full of ash trees
Ashenhurst – *AngloSaxon*	The hill with the ash trees
Ball Haye Green – *Norman French – Dieulacres Abbey*	A beautiful enclosure with a village green
Basford – *AngloSaxon*	Beoreol's (personal name) ford or the ford by the birch trees
Blackshaw – *Middle English*	The small, black wood
Blore – *AngloSaxon*	A high, windy place
Brund – *Unknown celtic or speculative AngloSaxon*	Fire or flame
Butterton – *AngloSaxon*	Hill used for production of butter
Calton – *AngloSaxon*	The farmstead where calves are reared
Castern – *AngloSaxon*	Caet's (personal name) thorn bush
Cheadle – *Old British/ AngloSaxon*	The clearing in Ced Wood ('ced' Old British for wood)
The Cloud – *AngloSaxon*	A rock ('clud')
Consall – *AngloSaxon*	A corner in a deep valley
Cotton – *AngloSaxon*	Cottages
The Dane (river) – *Old British*	A drop
Denford – *AngloSaxon*	The fold in the valley
The Dove (river) – *AngloSaxon*	To dive
Dunwood – *AngloSaxon*	The wood on the hill
Easing – *AngloSaxon*	The place or pasture of Ese (personal name)
Easing – *Very Speculative*	The holy place of ES (pagan god)
Elkstone – *AngloSaxon*	Ealac's (personal name) hill
Ellastone – *AngloSaxon*	Eadlac's (personal name) settlement
Farley – *AngloSaxon*	A fern covered clearing in a wood
Grindon – *AngloSaxon*	The green hill
The Hamps – *Old British* ('hafhesp')	Summer dry
Hollinsclough – *Middle English*	The ravine full of holly trees
Horton – *AngloSaxon*	Muddy settlement
Ilam – *AngloSaxon*	In the hills
Kingsley – *AngloSaxon*	The King's (royal) clearing

Longnor – *AngloSaxon*	The long ridge
River Manifold – *AngloSaxon*	Having many folds
Mixon – *AngloSaxon*	Dunghill
Musden – *AngloSaxon*	The valley infested with mice
Okeover – *AngloSaxon*	The steep slope where oak trees grow
Onecote – *AngloSaxon*	The lonely cottage
Quarnford – *AngloSaxon*	The mill by the ford
Ramshaw – *AngloSaxon*	The wood of the ram
Ramshorn – *AngloSaxon*	The ridge of the ram
Rownall – *AngloSaxon*	Rough nook or corner
Rudyard – *AngloSaxon*	The enclosure growing rue
Rushton – *AngloSaxon*	The settlement by the rushes
Sheen – *Old Norse*	A shed or shelter
Stanley – *AngloSaxon*	A stony clearing
Stanshope – *AngloSaxon*	The enclosed stony valley
Stanton – *AngloSaxon*	A settlement on stony ground
Swinscoe – *AngloSaxon &* *Old Norse*	The pig's wood – 'skogr' Old Norse for 'wood'
Throwley – *AngloSaxon*	A clearing near a deep valley
Tittesworth – *AngloSaxon*	The enclosed homestead of Tete (personal name)
Totmonslow – *AngloSaxon*	The burial mound of Tatmann (personal name)
Warslow – *AngloSaxon*	The burial mound of Wer (personal name) *or* the watch/look-out mound
Wetton – *AngloSaxon*	The wet hill
Whiston – *AngloSaxon*	Wita's (personal name) settlement
Wootton – *AngloSaxon*	The settlement by the wood

THE NAMING OF 'LEEK'

We now come on to the most important point, the actual naming of Leek itself.

'Leek' was given its name by the Saxon/Vikings, and we still use it today. So, just exactly what does the word 'LEEK' mean.

The Saxon name for a 'SPRING' or 'STREAM' was 'LAECC' (soft pronunciation), The Viking pronunciation of this word was 'LOEKR' (hard pronunciation).

To the Vikings a 'LOEKR' was a leak from the sacred Earth'. They believed as their long-boats leaked and let in salty water from the powerful sea, so Mother Earth leaked and gave out her pure, life-giving water.

In ancient documents it was written by the scribes as it was pronounced by our Saxon ancestors, 'LEC' - today we write it as 'LEEK' (hard Viking pronunciation).

WHY LEEK WAS NAMED AFTER A 'SPRING'.

Why, we need to ask, did our ancient ancestors name our town after a spring or sacred 'leak' in the earth?

To answer this we need to understand how our Saxon/Viking Leek ancestors perceived the world around them. In their verses they describe the moon as,

'A curious creature radiant sky rider richly adorned bearing booty between its horns'.

Fish were known as, **'The silver weed of the sea'.**

Their beliefs, their very culture, were totally centred around all the visible workings of Nature. The whole society from the King down to the slave depended for its wealth and survival on fertile land, good harvests, healthy animals and most importantly, a pure, continuous supply of water. We are not talking here about rivers which could become turgid during storms or dry during drought, but about wells and fresh water springs - And Leek during the Saxon/Viking era was blessed with just that.

PIGS FORAGING — TAKEN FROM ANGLOSAXON CALENDAR.
© *COPYRIGHT 1995 SAXON VILLAGE PROJECT*

The Spring was considered central to life. Both the Saxons and the later Viking settlers had a 'Sacramental' view of both wells and springs. They were frequently used for the blessing and healing of both humans and animals. It is known that the Pagan Saxons dipped their sick and infirm,

'3 times in the pool below a spring then 3 times against the Sun'.

This ritual was always associated with the number 3 or 9, which of course is related to the different phases of the moon. This ceremony continued on throughout the later Saxon Christian times.

Spring was the time for the dressing of the 'Goddess of the Water Spring' with flowers and dark greenery. This extremely ancient Anglo-Saxon custom still continues today in the Well-dressing ceremonies in Staffordshire and Derbyshire.

The Christian church over time replaced the old names of the pagan Goddesses of the well and spring with the names of Christian saints.

An Anglo-Saxon verse written at the time praises, 'Water'. The words are rich and beautiful and convey the very powerful feelings held by the Saxons in regard to their natural world. Translated, part of it reads,

'A cruel, fierce creature lives on Earth, her birth a miracle, her motion strong, she roars savagely and sweeps the ground. She is the Mother of many things, running serenely, ever restless, deep embracing. Her beauty and nature no man can express in words...adorned with treasure, dear to heroes. Her power grows...her beauty is honoured with favours of the world's glorious gems...To the rich, precious, priceless to the poor...Mother of the world's children...She is harder than Earth, older than heroes, greater than gifts, dearer than jewels...Men upon Earth must marvel at Her..'

WE NOW COME ON TO A VERY IMPORTANT POINT - Because the development of a village in past times depended on a pure water supply, and because natural sources of water held such a prominent place in the lives of the local population, <u>wells and springs were used during the Saxon period as a way of recording the landscape at a time when no maps existed. Many place-names in England owe their origins to these (Saxon) natural features.</u>

The Leek Spring

Among the many springs in Leek which existed at that time, one was very special. This spring 'leaked' from a spot in the earth considered both holy and unique by our Anglo Saxon and Viking ancestors; a place where could be seen a double sunset on Midsummer's Day, on which may well have stood a Bronze Age Burial Low, then a simple Christian Saxon church with its carved stone Saxon Crosses.

What an irresistible place it must have been for our Leek ancestors. One can easily imagine how such a spring would have been revered at a time when natural sources of pure water were considered hallowed places by Pagan and Christian alike.

You can still see the site of this Spring today — the very spring from which Leek derived its name. It is set on the side of the wall of St. Edward's Churchyard in Church Street Leek, and a lion's head now marks the spot.

In naming our town after this spring, the Saxons and later the Vikings were sending out a deliberate message. They were telling everyone loudly, both then and now,

"Here is an ancient place, a revered holy place, with a continuous supply of fresh, pure water given to us by the sacred Mother Earth and God the Maker."

Historians have noted that some of the very oldest springs in England are usually to be found 'half in and half out' of ancient churchyards, in other words, actually set in the churchyard wall, and are related to age old ceremonial sites.

Today, Man has become quite contemptuous of Nature and the natural world. He no longer has need of powerful Gods or the **magic of Creation.** He has a new God, the god of science and technology. In his desire to make money, to industrialise and develop his surroundings, he destroys much of his beautiful natural world; the trees, the animals and much of his sacred heritage. Yet despite all this, the timeless message of our ancestors remains safely hidden away in simple place-names such as, 'Leek'.

Many will know that the townspeople were still drinking from the Leek Spring as late as the 1950's, when a small tin mug attached to a chain hung alongside. Sadly, the water supply to it has now dried up due to centuries of urbanisation, then industrialisation of the town and finally the cutting off of the natural water supply by 20th century drainage systems.

THE LEEK SPRING

Drawing by Harry M. Ball

THE LEEK SPRING — 'LAECC' 'LOEKR' 'LEC' 'LEEK' (VIKING PRONUNCIATION) '- IS SET
IN THE WALL OF THE ST. EDWARD'S CHURCHYARD. THIS IS THE ACTUAL HOLY SPRING
AFTER WHICH THE TOWN WAS NAMED BY THE LEEK ANGLO SAXONS.
A PLAQUE SHOULD NOW BE RAISED THERE TO MARK THIS UNIQUE AND SPECIAL PLACE
AND AN ANNUAL CEREMONY OF BLESSING HELD EVERY MAY TIME IN KEEPING WITH LEEK'S
ANCIENT ANGLO SAXON/VIKING HERITAGE.

The Ancient Holy Wells and Springs of Leek

Leek, because of its geographical location, was once blessed with numerous pure water wells and sprngs. Indeed, Leek derives its name from one of these springs. Sadly, most are now 'lost' due to modern drainage schemes, road and housing development.

Our ancient Leek ancestors greatly valued those crystal clear waters and found them a source of healing, a place of devotion.

Throughout the decades, however, Leek's elected councillors have gained a poor reputation in that they have never fully appreciated the true value of such ancient, historical sites - now today's generation is paying the price. Hence the despair and anger over the 'official desecration' of the holy well in 'Ladydale'.

In complete contrast towns such as Buxton, and even some local moorland villages, have carefully protected their historic wells and openly encourage tourists to visit them – So fully exploiting the tourism potential of the area.

The 'Sainte Cene' Well

The 'Sainte Cene' Well *(place name Norman/French)* or 'The Well of the Holy Supper' is situated at 'Wall Grange' and was likely to have been the main water supply for the Roman fort which was located there. *(see the chapter on Roman Leek)*. It was described by John Sleigh in the 1800's as 'a most copious, pellucid (crystalline) spring'.

Wall Grange, described in the past as a *'domus defensabilis' or 'a defended house'* and consisting of about 500 acres, was given to Trentham Priory by the Norman Earl of Chester. There are several holy wells in Normandy, France that carry the name of 'Sainte Cene'. The name became corrupted here over the centuries, some mistakingly calling it 'Sinner's / Coenose's Well', because our Leek ancestors were unable to pronounce the French name.

The 'Wall Grange' well was given its special Christian name by the Priory because, at that time, fresh water springs /wells were used as places of blessing, healing and celebration – the Last Supper was an occasion of blessing and celebration for Jesus and his Apostles.

We have no documented evidence to show if it carried a different Saxon name previous to this. In 1847 it was 'appropriated to the Potteries Water Works'!

'LADY (Hlaefdige) DALE' or 'OUR LADY OF THE DALE'

'Lady Dale' Well is situated in the area known as 'Lady Dale' close to Cheddleton Road. This holy name was given to the well and its surrounding area during early mediaeval times by the Christian Church. The place name is AngloSaxon and comes directly from 'hlaefdige' which is pronounced similar to /and means - 'lady'. The title was only ever given to either the wife of the King (example – 'Our Lady of the Mercians') or to the Holy Mother of Jesus.

'Hlaefdige' translated from the AngloSaxon means, 'loaf kneader' – 'hlaef' meaning loaf, 'dige' meaning 'to knead'. This was an important title as the King or Lord's title was 'Hlaefhorde' or 'the keeper (hoarder) of the loaf'. The 'loaf' being a symbolic word of Lordship.

In the case of 'Lady Dale' the word refers exclusively to Our Lady, the Mother of Jesus. However it is likely, as was often the case, that the name replaced an earlier name dedicated to a pagan goddess of the well. For example this occurred at St. Ann's well in Buxton.

The name shows that the well was held in high esteem in both early and late Christian worship. It was seen as a place of healing and pilgrimage. In the 1700's the words 'Lady o' the Dale' had been corrupted into 'Laddermedale' due to local pronunciation.

There are still those living today who took part in the processions from St. Mary's R.C. Church to the holy well. They tell us that the ceremony was held in May. The statue of Mary in the church was crowned with a wreath of fresh flowers. Jesus's Mother was then given the title, 'Queen of Angels, Queen of the May'. The procession proceeded on down to the 'Lady Dale' Well for a ceremony of blessing in honour of Our Lady.

The present Church has a religious duty to revive this ancient and holy tradition (one that was held in high regard by the early Christian church) and to 'reclaim' the Well in the name of Mary. It is still a holy and dedicated place, and will always continue to be so. Many Christians in the town of Leek believe those who mar the beauty of the Well and its Dale, in the pursuit of gain and profit, are defiling the very name of Our Lady.

THE 'EGG WELL'. – 'egg' the original Viking word for egg.

The 'Egg Well' is situated at Ashenhurst, nr. Bradnop. We cannot be certain of the true meaning of the name because of lack of documented evidence. Possibilities include, 'Egga's Well' (a personal place name) or the name could be a corruption of an ancient term, now lost, that did not relate to the modern word 'egg'. An oval, elliptical 'egg shaped' stone bowl was built to enclose the water supply. But which came first the chicken or the egg?! Was the stone surround built that way because the unusual name already existed or did the word come into use later as a direct result of the egg shaped stone bowl?

However, names aside, it is evident that the water from the well has been greatly valued for its curative properties over many, many centuries. In the early 1800's the Roman Catholic Priest, the Rev. Samual Whittaker, translated the Latin inscription which had been carved there by William Stanley in the 1700's. The translation read, *The racking stone its tortured victim leaves: Spleen, heart and liver ailments cease – A thousand evils own this water's power'.*

THE BUXTON ROAD SPRINGS

In the early 1800's an important source of drinking water was wells and springs. Many Leek residents collected their water in wooden buckets from the freshwater springs which flowed, even in times of drought, from the green hillsides by Buxton Road and the present Springfield Road. The modern day Adam's Butter factory was unfortunately built over the top of a particularly fine, pure water spring.

How carelessly we discard Nature's gifts!

THE 'LEEK' *'Lec'* *'Laecc'* *'Loekr'* SPRING

The 'Leek' Spring (from which Leek derived its name) is located on the outer wall of St. Edward's Church. Although now dry due to modern Man's activities it is, in 'place-name terms' the most unique and important spring in the whole of the Staffordshire Moorlands and Derbyshire. The name 'Leek' 'Lec' 'Laecc' is AngloSaxon / 'Loekr' Viking - and means 'a spring, stream a holy leak from the earth'. A full description of this spring, its history and its great importance to the town is fully covered in the Saxon/Viking chapter.

There are, no doubt, many other old wells and springs that could be added to the above list by the people of the Leek Moorlands.

It is now imperative that Leek revives the ancient spring and well dressing ceremonies that surely took place at least as far back as AngloSaxon times. We owe to it our children and our children's children to uphold the ancient traditions of our town, and to celebrate the history of the special, holy spring that gave Leek its name.

'Time consecrates: And what is grey with Age becomes Religion'
Frederick von Schiller'

THE LEEK SPRING IN SAXON TIMES

ᛋᚲᚱᛁᛏᚷ Runic spelling of 'Spring'

The 'holy' Spring which flowed at the time of the Leek Saxons was a far more wondrous thing than our parents and grandparents would ever remember.

For a start, the level of the water table in the underground sandstone beds was much higher than it is today, so that a powerful head of water literally gushed out of the sandstone hill on which St. Edward's Church now stands.

Gallons and gallons of this pure, life-giving element filled a deep pool and fed a wide stream which flowed freely down a natural channel on the site of the present day Mill Street, and then on down into the River Churnet.

In later centuries, this stream was diverted along a man-made channel into Spout Street, now called St. Edward's Street.

THERE WOULD MOST CERTAINLY HAVE BEEN A CEREMONY OF BLESSING IN THOSE PAST TIMES, ONE THAT HAS SADLY BEEN FORGOTTEN.

However, we need little imagination to picture the everyday Leek scene-

The Saxon/Viking women beside the spring filling their brown, hand-thrown pots with sparkling water for cooking and the brewing of mead ; the richly dressed Saxon Lord, his Sheriff and their tall noble Warriors resplendent with swords and armour, watering their proud horses; the talkative Viking merchants and weary pilgrims grateful for the cool refreshment; the early Saxon pagans gathering together in Maytime, paying respect to the Goddess of the spring, then the Christians with their Priests, baptising converts, blessing the sick and praying to the new Christian Saints.

We can only wonder what other ancient ceremonies took place there at the time of Spring, Harvest, Midwinter (*middanwinter*) and especially Midsummer (*middansummer*) when the giant red sun set twice behind The Cloud and set the moorland hills alight with fiery glow.

The Time is now ripe for the people of Leek to raise a plaque to mark this hallowed site. They should also come together each May-time to hold a ceremony of blessing at the Spring which gave Leek its name. No other village or town in this area can claim such a special or unique place-name. We owe it to our children and our children's children to keep alive the memory, history and traditions of our ancient Leek ancestors.

It is a sad reflection on our education system that the children of Iceland and Germany know more about the Saxon history of England, which of course includes Leek, than do the children of England.

Another ancient natural source of water exists in the town, this is the well at 'LADYDALE. The name is Anglo Saxon. It means, "Our Lady's Dale' and it refers to the Mother of Christ, as in 'LADY MEADOWS' at Bottom House. However, it is very likely 'Lady Dale' had an even older pre-Christian name, one of a Pagan Saxon Goddess. This site should be preserved at all costs from the attentions of any housing developers.
(see pages on Leek's Ancient wells and springs)

WHAT DID LEEK LOOK LIKE IN SAXON/VIKING TIMES?

We now know what the Leek Spring looked like, but what about the rest of the village. Again we need to picture the scene.

.... On the sandstone rise above the Leek Spring stands a small wooden or half stone thatched church, plus a number of tall, carved Saxon stone crosses. Close to the church are clusters of wooden houses and buildings. The roofs are expertly and attractively thatched with reeds. Each dwelling has a 'WYRTYEARD' or 'yard' in which grow herbs and vegetables such as 'MINTAN' - mint, 'SALVIE' - sage, 'RAEDIC' - radish, 'SLARGIE' - clary.

Built at the edge of the present day Market Place, is a long Saxon Hall where the people meet together for ceremonies, story telling and feasting. At such feasts oat cakes, very like the ones we eat today are served, as well as stone-ground bread and cheese, honey cakes, mushrooms, roasted game and a great variety of vegetables. The men, women and children drink beer, mead and apple juice.
On the present site of the Red Lion stands the Lord's Manor House, and close by the specially built barn for the 'food-rent'.

Over in the West, in the flatter areas we now call West Street, Field Street and The Westwood Recreation Ground, are open fields laid out in strips where farmers are ploughing with oxen and heavy wooden ploughs. There they grow wheat for bread, onions, carrots, beans, peas, cabbage, celery, spinach and leeks. Beside the fields,

71

standing proud, the ancient Bronze Age Burial Mounds, including 'Cock Low".

On the higher surrounding hillsides, cattle, pigs, goats and sheep graze freely. Young village boys armed with bows and arrows act as shepherds, along with their powerful dogs who keep away the wolves. The rushing, hillside streams which tumble down from the heather-clad moors are full of water-cress - our Saxon ancestors eat this in great quantities.

The River Churnet wends its way through the valley below. The deep water is clean, sparkling and full of darting fish. Some villagers are down there now in small wooden boats, fishing with long lines and sharp bone hooks.

In the distance, you can just catch the sound of a hunting horn. The men are out with their hawks and hunting dogs.

The view from Leek is green and beautiful. All around the village are acres and acres of mixed woodland. - <u>This was 'The Great Wood of Leek'</u>.......

THE GREAT WOOD OF LEEK.

This wood is recorded in the later Norman 'Domesday Book'. It measured four leagues by four leagues. As a League at that time was one and a half miles, then the trees covered thirty six square miles. Compared to many other Manors at that time, it was a very large wood.

For place-name evidence of this great wood we only need to look at the Saxon name 'LEEKFRITH', for the word 'frith' means 'woodland' . There is also, 'WESTWOOD', 'HILLSWOOD', 'THORNCLIFF', 'WETWOOD' and 'ALDERLEE' which means ' a clearing in the wood'.

The word, 'SHAW' is the Old English word for 'copse' or 'thicket', and so we have the names, 'BLACKSHAW', 'RAMSHAW', 'REDSHAW', and 'SHAWBANK'.

Finally there are the names, 'BACK FOREST' and 'HIGH FOREST' which are beyond the Roaches. These would have marked the boundry of the Great Wood.

This vast woodland area not only extended to the North and West of Leek, but also to the South and East. So we find the names, 'BIRCHALL' and 'ASHENHURST', which means, 'the hillock covered in ash trees'.

11TH CENT. ANGLOSAXON WOODCUTTERS
© COPYRIGHT 1995 SAXON VILLAGE PROJECT

These ancient place-names were written down as early as 1129, 1250, through the 1200's AD as well as the 14th and 15th. centuries. They give clear evidence of the type of trees which grew then. There are references to 'oaks', 'birches', 'ashes', 'thorns' and even 'hollies'.

This Great Wood provided the people of Leek with timber to build their houses, tools, furniture and fuel for their fires.

The presence of so many trees is given strong support by a scientific analysis of pollen still present in the local peat beds close to Leek.

In 1976 a boring was made by scientists into the peat deposits north of 'Meerbrook' and in the middle of 'Leekfrith'. In the higher levels of peat going down to the 13th. century, there were only pollens of grasses and sedges. This showed evidence of only pasture land, whereas in the lower, older levels going back to Saxon times and before, the pollen came from the trees mentioned above.

BIRDLIFE DURING SAXON TIMES.

The woodlands and hills around the town were full of rich birdlife such as Nightingales which the Saxons called, '*Nihtegale*', Mistle Thrush or '*Scric*', Green Woodpecker or '*Higere*', - And it would not have been an uncommon thing to see a Vulture or '*Earn Geap*' fly across the hills, because Vultures existed in England at that time.

 We know that the Saxons took a special interest in the bird life which surrounded them. They named the Lapwing a '*Hlaepwince*' or a 'Leap Winker', this is because they had noted how the black and white feathers appeared to 'wink' black to white as the bird hopped and flew along.

The Anglo-Saxon Chronicles, which reserved much of its writings for the activities of Kings and battles, dire deeds and the recording of unusual events such as the appearance of comets, noted in the year 671 AD that, '*This year there was a great*

mortality of birds'. This was probably due to a severe winter.

A riddle was written by an Anglo-Saxon which described a bird. Can you tell which bird the riddle was referring to.

This air carries little creatures over hillsides,

They are very bright, black, dark coated,

Rich with song, they roam in flocks, cry loudly,

Tread woody headlands, even in the halls of men,

They name themselves.........?'

(answer ...SWALLOWS)

The Leek Moorlands would have been a paradise for all kinds of wildlife in Saxon/Viking times. The River Churnet then was pure and unpolluted, Nature was feared and respected.

How different it is today. Not one of the green fields, trees or even wild creatures around our ancient town are really safe from misguided planners and avaricious property developers with their destructive earth-moving equipment and large bank accounts. Leek's precious heritiage is being systematically destroyed.

VIKING V SAXON

The Vikings who settled in the Leek Moorlands were mainly Danes, some were also of mixed Scandinavian origin.

By the time they arrived they were to settle down peacefully amongst the local Saxons. However, the history of the long relationship between the Saxon aristocracy of England and the Vikings is a long and complicated affair.

For a time the Vikings would hold sway over the land, then the Saxons. The Viking army actually held Derby for a while and made it a Viking stronghold. But, as mentioned earlier, the town was later freed by King's Alfred's Grandaughter.

'DERBY' is a Viking name and means 'Deer Farm'. Before Viking times it was called, NORTHWORTHING' by the Anglo Saxons.

ANGLOSAXON HUNTING WITH A HAWK
©SAXON VILLAGE PROJECT

74

In England there are hundreds of hybrid Scandinavian/Anglo Saxon place names. Some of the towns and villages with Saxon/Viking names are actually on sites settled during the time of the Roman occupation. Saxon/Viking and Roman archaeological remains may well still lie undiscovered beneath Leek itself.

THE RELIGION OF THE LEEK VIKINGS

When the Vikings first arrived in our area they were pagans, while the Saxons were Chrisitians.

The Vikings worshipped gods such as **JOTNUS** - the Dark Giant, and **ASAS** - the Friendly God. Then there was **AEGIR** - he was a Sea Giant who controlled the storms, and **NIORD** - the Sea God who protected ship while they were still in harbour.

The Vikings believed that their Gods lived in a wonderful city called **ASGARD.** In this city there was a great Hall - It had pillars of gold and a roof of silver. When they died they were judged for their good or bad deeds in a place called **GLINIR.**

In the early days of the invasion the Vikings frequently raided Christian churches for their gold and altar goods; religious books were burnt and destroyed, priests murdered. Thankfully, there is no evidence of similar events in this area. By the 10th. century, the Vikings had adopted some of the beliefs of Christianity. They began to raise stone slabs and crosses for their dead carved with runic inscriptions.

During this Saxon/Viking era thousands of Christian churches were built on older religious sites - And many Christian rural parishes were formed.

The landowners encouraged this because churches were looked on as a status symbol. The Saxon/Viking aristocracy began burying their dead in churchyards surrounding the church, rather than in burial mounds. These burials differed from the older pagan burials in that no grave goods were placed alongside the dead. Because of this fact, it is sometimes difficult to give a precise date to excavated Christian burial sites. Dating sometimes had to depend on remains of clothing or jewellery being found by chance.

SAXON COPED TOMB — ORNAMENTED WITH ANIMALS, HORSE, ELEPHANTS, DEER & TREE. — BAKEWELL CHURCH IN DERBYSHIRE. — THOMAS BATEMAN

THE BLOCKED UP NORTH DOOR – ST. EDWARD'S CHURCH

This photograph shows the now blocked up northern door of the ancient mediaeval church of St. Edwards – Leek. The very early Saxon churches were built with a 'north door' to the Nave. Architecturally, however, they had little significance in regard to use, but were constructed for 'religious' purposes. The Christian Church 'carried over' many of the pagan beliefs of the Saxons. One of these was that North was connected to the Saxon God, 'Woden'. So the northern door of a church was called 'The Devil's Door' in Norman and Mediaeval times. The North side of the church was known as 'the sinister side' (*Latin – sinestre means 'left'*).

We know that during infant baptisms it was opened so that, 'evil spirits could escape' when they were sent out of the child by the priest. When it was not being used for various rituals, such as 'churching' of women after having a child, it was kept locked. Many of these doors were eventually blocked up by the Church.

It is extremely likely that Saxon/Viking Christian burials exist within the the present-day church yard of St. Edward's Church. Excavation of the church yard would probably bring to light archaeological remains. However, it is unlikely ever to happen as the sanctity of any burial site, especially in a churchyard must always at all times be respected.

The present church of St. Edwards would originally have been a Saxon/Viking stone/wooden building, which was later rebuilt during Norman times.

GOOD AND EVIL

As said before, the Christian religion dovetailed with the earlier Saxon Pagan beliefs.

The Saxon/Viking Christians still worshipped the Sun, Moon, Springs and even Stones. The Christian ceremonies were carried out by priests, most of whom had previously been Pagan priests called, 'Ealdorbiscop'.

This legacy is still with us today. Christian prayers and texts, which have been handed down through the centuries, are rich and colourful and refer to the sun, moon, life giving fountains of water, trees and birds to mention but a few.

When one looks at the old Saxon Christian stone crosses, one is able to see a very close relationship between Pagan and Christian beliefs.

Mercia had, and still has, a wealth of carved stones, especially within the area of the Peak District. This may be due to the fact that here there is a plentiful supply of stone which is both suitable for carving and is also long lasting.

Mercia also had its own special style of crosses. From 750 to 800 AD, the crosses were of an Anglo-Saxon design. From 900 to 1050 AD the style of carving shows a definite Scandinavian influence.

MAN FIGHTING MYTHICAL BEASTS ANGLOSAXON c.625 GOLD,
GARNET & GLASS PURSE DECORATION
© 1995 SAXON VILLAGE PROJECT

THE LEEK CALVARY STONE

The Calvary Stone in Leek St. Edward's churchyard depicts a figure carrying a long, cross shaped 'weapon' which is being used to kill a serpent or dragon. Some have said it is the figure of Christ carrying his cross to Calvary. However, it is extremely difficult to differentiate between the figure of Christ and the old Pagan Hero who often went out to kill dragons and serpents.

The Serpent or Dragon for both Saxon/Viking Christian and Pagan alike represented Evil. We cannot be sure if the figure on the stone is holding a cross or a sword, because Saxon battle swords were extremely long, splended objects.

However, if one reads old Saxon texts, it becomes plain that it would have mattered little to our Saxon/Viking Leek ancestors. For them the Pagan Hero overcoming Evil, and Christ the Redeemer were fulfilling one and the same function.

In fact the Cross was a pagan symbol prior to Christianity. It was also a very common symbol of both Fire and the Sun.

The Christian church in later times attempted to give Paganism a bad name, connecting it wrongly with human sacrifice and satanism. The Church even went so far as to portray the God Oden as the Devil.

In reality, the old Saxon/Viking pagans were extremely respectful of the God or Gods of Creation. In venerating trees, springs and the Earth they were in fact worshipping the Creator.

They cared for, often feared, the natural world around them, knowing full well it was a living manifestation of the power of a great Creator.

They had no comprehension of Satan, only good and evil, light and darkness. The Fallen Angel Satan, the Devil and Satanism were in fact a Christian 'invention'.

All good pagans expected and wished for Good to triumph over Evil, Light to overcome Darkness - That is why their ancient stories and legends are full of great heros who fought only on the side of Good.

This mixture of both Christian and Pagan belief was to continue in England through Norman times and up to the present day. The northern door of Christian Anglo-Saxon churches were often blocked up by the French Christian Normans after 1066 and the Norman invasion, because it was thought that the north door of a church was still the God Woden's door. The altar was always put on the East side of the church, the same side as the rising Sun.

77

The Leek Calvary Stone

DRAWING BY HARRY M. BALL

WHEN OUR LEEK ANGLO SAXON ANCESTORS
TOOK ON THE CHRISTIAN RELIGION, THEY DID
NOT IN THE STRICT SENSE OF THE WORD
'CONVERT', BUT ADAPTED THE 'NEW' RELIGION
TO ACCOMMODATE THEIR OWN DEEPLY ROOTED
PAGAN BELIEFS. ENGLISH CHRISTIANITY TODAY
CONTAINS MANY PAGAN REFERENCES, ELEMENTS
AND CUSTOMS.

THE ANGLO SAXONS PREFERRED & IDENTIFIED WITH
THE OLD TESTAMENT STORIES IN THE BIBLE. THEY
SAW THEM AS AN EXTENSION OF THEIR OWN
HEROIC TRADITIONS - THOSE OF GODS, HEROES,
DRAGONS & GOOD FIGHTING EVIL.

WHEN THEY RECOUNTED THE STORIES FROM THE OLD
TESTAMENT THEY THOUGHT NOTHING OF ADDING ON
AN IMAGINARY BATTLE AND THEIR 'TRANSLATIONS'
SOMETIMES READ LIKE ANCIENT PAGAN SAGAS.
OLD TESTAMENT WOMEN, SUCH AS RUTH,
WERE PORTRAYED AS 'SHIELD MAIDENS', AND
THE ANGLOSAXON STORY OF EXODUS HAS MOSES
ACCOMPANIED BY 'THANES' (ANGLO SAXON WARRIORS).

THE IDEA OF A SACRIFICIAL CHRIST DID NOT APPEAL TO THEM.
THEY ADMIRED AN ALL POWERFUL, FIERY GOD. THEY
STILL REFERRED TO THE GOD WODEN AS 'THE ALL FATHER',
WHILE AT THE SAME TIME CALLING THE CHRISTIAN GOD, 'THE MAKER'.
THIS IS REFLECTED IN THE ILLUSTRATION ON THE LEEK CALVARY STONE. SOME HAVE CLAIMED IT IS
CHRIST CARRYING THE CROSS, YET WE CAN CLEARLY MAKE OUT THE GIANT MYTHICAL SERPENT THAT
FEATURED EXTENSIVELY IN ANGLOSAXON/VIKING PAGAN RELIGION. THE CARVING DEPICTS A HERO
OVERCOMING A SERPENT OR 'WORM' (DRAGON). WE ALSO NEED TO EXAMINE 'THE CROSS'. THE STONE
MASON AT THE TIME WOULD HAVE KNOWN ABOUT THE CHRISTIAN STORY OF CALVARY - BUT THE CROSS
IS MORE LIKELY, JUDGING BY ITS PROPORTIONS, DESIGN AND SIZE, TO BE A LONG SAXON SWORD THAT
IS BEING USED TO KILL THE MYTHICAL CREATURE WHICH REPRESENTS 'EVIL' - EXACTLY IN THE SAME WAY
AS THE ANGLO SAXONS DEPICTED THEIR PAGAN HEROES! THE DEVIL HIMSELF DID NOT & STILL DOES NOT
'EXIST' IN PAGAN RELIGION — HE WAS IN FACT A CHRISTIAN 'INVENTION'.
THE LEEK ANGLO SAXON PAGANS HAD GREAT RESPECT FOR THEIR GODS AND THE NATURAL WORLD —
THEY WISHED ONLY FOR LIGHT TO CONQUER DARKNESS.

Despite our ancestors being Christian the old beliefs still remained. One AngloSaxon Christian prayer actually said, 'Hail to thee Earth, Mother of Men. Be thou fruitful of God's existence'. In the same breath, the Saxons were speaking to both Mother Earth & the Christian God. On other occasions when praying they would speak of 'Magic' or 'scinncraeft' which could supposedly conjure up a 'shining phantom'. When they recited the prayer, 'Our Father', they would speak of Christ and his mother Mary as' standing over disease of every kind' and in the same line speak of Woden and his fight against Evil'. The name 'Woden' actually means, 'Master of Inspiration'. It is connected to the word, 'wod' (old English) which means, 'poetic inspiration'. The Norse god counterpart, Odinn', held a treasure called, Aegishjalmr' which translated means, 'the helmet of terror'.

THOR' , the pagan god of war and smithery , was often portrayed as carrying a fiery hot hammer. The Saxon/Viking pagans wore a hammer sign called, Thor's Hammer' around their necks and they used it to 'trace the air with the sign of blessing'. During Christian times this very hammer became 'fused' with the cross of Christ, and was still used in an identical way to give a blessing. Our pagan Saxon ancestors believed that a 'third eye' existed in the centre of the forehead which gave men insight into the world of heaven and eternity. Christians today still touch the site of this 'third eye' when they sign themselves with the sign of the cross.

THE GREEN MAN

Everyone in England is familiar with the traditions of 'Morris Dancing'. This ritual, unique to England, dates from the ancient Anglo Saxon celebration of Spring. & 'The Green Man' who was the God of the English Anglo Saxon people - He was known as, 'ING'.

He actually had his own Rune Sign shown here ..... ᛝ

AngloSaxon verse stated, 'ING was first seen among the East Danes. He then went Westwards across the waves following his waggon. Thus so the warriors named the Hero'.

This is one of the very early references to what was the migration of the 'English' or 'Engle' from Angelin in Schleswig, Holstein to this country & eventually to Leek. In the 'Morris Dance' there is the stamping of feet;this is meant to awaken the sleeping God, 'Ing', who in turn awakens Nature. The high leaping and dancing represents the growing up of the crops. The Green Man is often portrayed as a 'vegetation god' – his face is always framed by greenery. Other Anglo Saxon names of him are, 'Lord of the Wood', 'The Stag God', 'The Horned God', and 'Lord of the Animals'. People sometimes mistakenly relate this green god to other non Anglo-Saxon pagan religions, But Ing, The Green Man is a purely English Saxon God.

RUNES – ᚠᛗᛗᚪ ᚱᚾᛏᛗᚻ

We know from local archaeological evidence that the Leek Anglo Saxons/Vikings used Runes. In fact Runes were first introduced into England by the Saxons and were a Germanic form of writing called the, 'Futhhore'. The word, 'write' is an AngloSaxon word which means, 'To scratch Runes on a (tree) bark'. **These runes only existed in Germany, England, Sweden, Iceland and Scandinavia. There have never been any Welsh or Irish Runes.** Runes were 'male' symbols and were originally connected with warriors, heroes and fighting tradition. Each one represented a symbolic element of life.

The first rune ᚠ. feo refers to the Norse creation story which includes a cow. During those early times wealth could be measured by how many cows a man owned, so 'feo' came to represent WEALTH. It is as simple as that.

The second rune ᚢ. ur represents AUROCHS, a strong and powerful wild cow of ancient Europe, which sadly became extinct in the 17th century. ᚢ ur therefore represents 'STRENGTH'.

The third rune, Thorn. Th. represents the Giant THURS, which is a version of the God, THOR and is connected to the THORN TREE. The Thorn stands for powerful protection in the same way as the tree protects itself with sharp thorns on its branches....And so it continues. All the knowledge we have today on the meaning of the runes comes mainly from three Runic Poems. These poems are Icelandic, Norwegian and Anglo-Saxon.

79

THERE ARE ACTUALLY 31 ANGLO SAXON RUNES AND UP TO 24 VIKING RUNES. ᚦᚻᛖᚱᛖ ᚨᚱᛖ ᚨᚳᛏᚢᚨᛚᛚᚤ ⁝ ᛋᚨᛉᚨᚾᚱᚢᚾᛖᛋ

Runes were used in practical ways to mark a person's name on swords, rings and even a lady's comb. Sometimes they were used in magic and religious ceremonies, as well as for decorating gravestones and standing stones.

However, the Runes themselves hold no magic power, they are merely another form of writing which developed in an era when symbolism, ritual and folk-lore played a powerful part in everyday life.

What made them so special was the fact that only a small number of Anglo Saxons were able to read and decipher them. This gave the more learned of the Saxons a special knowledge, which in turn gave them a higher status within the community. To hold 'THE SECRET OF THE RUNES' was to hold the power of authority. This fact, no doubt, encouraged an elite band of Saxons to attach magical properties to Runes.

A belief in the 'MAGIC OF THE RUNES' was widespread amongst the Saxon/Viking nobility. The famous and wise, BEDE in his ancient writings tells the true story of the English Saxon Lord who was taken prisoner in the battle between Ecgfrith of Northumberland and Aethilred of Mercia (of which Leek was part). The Lord's bonds were supposed to have fallen off when his brother celebrated a Christian Mass while holding the magic Runes!

The ancient Hero BEOWULF was said to have, 'unbind the Rune of war'.

The casting of the Runes or 'lots' would have been accompanied by the reciting of spells or magical chants. In the 'Legend of St. Andrew' it says in Anglo Saxon, 'Hluton hellcraeftum haeden-gyldum' which means, 'They cast lots with hellish craft before the heathen gods'. +

When the Saxons turned to Christianity they began to use the Latin and Roman alphabet for their writings – And of course as might be expected, some of the first people to 'convert' to Christianity were the **Readers of the Runes.** These men cleverly transferred their loyalty from one religion to another, and in so doing were able to retain their authority as Priests amongst their own people.

ᛖ ᚨᚱᛖ ᛏᚻᛖ ᚨᚾᚷᛚᚨ ᛋᚨᛉᚨᚾᛋ ᚹᛖ ᚹᛁᛋᚻ ᚨᚾᛚᚤ ᚠᚨᚱ ᛖᚾᚷᛚᚨᚾᛞ ᛏᚨ ᛒᛖ ᚠᚱᛖᛖ

WE STILL USE ONE OF THE RUNES TODAY - when we put a cross sign on the bottom of a letter to denote friendship or affection.

Many books have been written on the subject of the Runes. Some are sensible and based on academic research plus a 'down to earth' appreciation of ancient belief and custom. Others are 'full of fancy' or just plain silly.

SAXON / VIKING WARRIORS

The time of the Saxon/Vikings was truly an heroic age. Loyalty to one's Lord, especially in battle, was paramount. Battles were usually fought on foot and fighting was. hand-to-hand using swords, spears, knives, bows, shields and axes.

Spears were considered to be weapons of Woden, and some of the spear-heads were inlaid with silver, gold and other precious metals.

Axes were known as Thor's Weapon', even in Christian times.

A wall of shields was often created to protect the warriors from a hail of arrows. Sometimes the shields would be weighed down with arrows and become too heavy to hold. The Saxon/Viking word for a shield was 'Spear Land'. Descriptive words such as 'Bow-drift' and 'Spear-storms' also formed part of the language. In later times, decorated shields began to be used for heraldic displays.

A sword was the most precious weapon of a Warrior. They were handed down from Father to Son. These weapons of war, so often decorated with silver animals, snakes and leaves, also demonstrated a man's wealth and position in society.

Along with rings and ships, swords were actually given names. 'Magic lurks in every name, bearing good or evil fame'. Hence the legendary name of 'EXCALIBER.

Swords were usually carried in a fur-lined scabbard decorated with gilt, bronze and runic inscriptions.

A poem written at the time when the Anglo-Saxons were attempting to fight off the Viking invasions, just after the battle on the banks of the River Blackwater in Essex, tell of the bravery of the warriors who fought there,

'Then the battle-wolves, the Viking hoards were not stopped by the water. Byrhtnoth with his men stood waiting. They let fly the file-hard spears —bows were busy, points pierced shields. Then Edward the Tall stood at the front of the battle – He broke down the Shield Wall and fought the Warriors until he had avenged the death of his Chief. Then Byrhtnoth drew his broad brown-edged sword from its sheath – the noble retainer Aetheric also fought boldly, then were the shields broken.'

We can but wonder just how many Warriors such as these lived in or visited the Lands of Leek in ancient times. The story of King Alfred's amazing life and adventures and those of other English Saxon Kings would outshine any modern-day Hollywood epic. Then there are the great many Saxon and Viking Heroes, numerous Earls and noble warriors' such as Byrhtnoth' whose names are never spoken by today's English children. The education of our young ones is sorely lacking in terms of the long and wonderfully rich history & culture of the English people before 1066 AD. In fact Byrhtnoth was a Saxon warrior who was famous not only for his noble deeds, but also because he was 6 feet 7 inches tall.

WHAT HAPPENED TO THE LEEK SAXONS & VIKINGS?

There is still so much that can be told about our Anglo Saxon ancestors – About their wonderful art and manuscripts, their jewellery which can be seen in various museums around the country. Much of the work is so fine and intricate it is almost impossible to believe that it was made by human hand and not by a modern machine! Then of course there is the famous tapestry work that was sought throughout the whole of Christendom. In fact, the English Anglo-Saxons created some of the most beautiful and dynamic art, crafts and literature in the whole of the world's history. They were highly civilised, brave and proud and had a finely developed sense of law, chivalry and justice. They deserve far greater recognition than is being given in today's education system. English children, unlike the Welsh, Scottish and Irish are actually being deliberately denied knowledge of their cultural heritage by misguided & intolerant adults working to a hidden & politically correct agenda.

> **As for the Saxon/Viking settlers of Leek – they never left. They are still here in our genes and culture, in our ancient traditions, our language – And of course in the name of the town of Leek.**

THE AGE OF CHIVALRY AND LEARNING

The first AngloSaxon English lived in the Staffordshire Moorlands within the kingdom of Mercia over twelve centuries ago, and yet their respectful manners and desire for civility would easily outshine many of our modern social customs.

We are able to see examples of this in documents written at that time. Below are a few extracts from letters penned in 796 AD to King Offa, who ruled over Mercia and the lands of Leek;

EXTRACTS FROM LETTERS SENT TO KING OFFA OF MERCIA IN 796 AD.

extract 1 - 'To the most excellent man and to us most dear, Offa, King of the Mercians, his humble friend Alcium sends greetings...Be it known..that the lord king, Charles, has often spoken to me of you in a most loving and loyal way. Thus is he sending envoys to Rome for the judgment of the apostolic pope and of Archbishop AEthelheard. He is also sending fitting gifts to you...'

extract 2 - letter from Charles the Great to King Offa 'Between royal dignities and exalted personages of the world, the keeping of the laws of friendship..is wont to be the profit to many...Concerning pilgrims..they may go in peace free from all molestation bearing with them the necessities for their journey...You have written to us about merchants..we allow that they shall have protection and support in our kingdom, lawfully according to the ancient custom of trading...Moreover we make known to your love that we have sent a gift..'

extract 3 - ' To the most excellent King Offa, Alcuin, a humble deacon, sends greeting...I have sent back to you this my most dear son, beseeching you to maintain him with honour.. Do not let him wander in idleness or take to drink, but provide him with pupils and strictly charge him to teach diligently..It greatly pleases me that you are so intent on education, that in the light of wisdom..may shine in your kingdom...You are the glory of Britain, the sword against foes, the shield against enemies. Do justice, love mercy, for he who forgives will be forgiven.'

Letter from Alciun to the Mercian Ealdormann Osbert.

'..Admonish all the race of the Mercians diligently to observe the good, moderate and chaste customs, which (king) Offa established for them that they may have..stability and strength for their kingdom against their enemies..and preach to the people in the piety of holy religion and set an example for good.
Live happily ..my dearest friend'.

The literary works of King Alfred.

King Alfred had the education and welfare of his people at heart when he made a selection from the works of the most eminent writers, including those from classical Rome. He had translated from Latin into AngloSaxon the best and most popular works of the time. Four of these were, 'The Compendious History of the World by Orosius', 'The Ecclesiastical History of Bede', 'The Consolations of Philosophy of Boethius', and 'Gregory's Pastoral Care'.

In these translations the King did not always follow the author's words exactly but used his freedom and exercised his own judgement to add remarks and illustrations. (As you can see from the illustration the King wrote in AngloSaxon script) But the longest and most important editions written by Alfred are in his translations of the Description of Europe and the voyages of two explorers called Ohthere and Wulfstan.

Ohthere made a voyage around Norway and the North Cape into the White Sea, while Wulfstan made a journey around the Baltic Sea. The King recorded the experiences of these ancient explorers, and his words made amazing reading. They describe the geography of Europe and give us insight into how the people lived at that time.

For example Alfred tells us that,

'Esthonia is very large and there are many towns, and in every town there is a king. There is also very much honey and fishing. The King and the richest men drink mare's milk (milk fermented into brandy) and the poor and the slaves drink mead...There is also among the Esthonians a power of producing cold; And if a man sets two vats full of ale or of water, they cause that either shall be frozen over, whether it be winter or summer. (This power which the King writes about refers to the use of ice-houses used to preserve food).

King Alfred says of AngloSaxon Britain,

'It extends a long way north-east. It is 8 hundred miles long and 2 hundred miles broad. On the south of it and on the other side of the arm of the sea is Gallia Belgica, and on the west part on the other side of the sea is the island of Hibernia and on the north part the Orkney islands. Ireland which we shall call Scotland is on every side surrounded by the ocean and because it is nearer to the setting of the sun than other lands the weather is milder there than in Britain. Then on the north-west of Ireland is that outmost land called Thule; and it is known to few because of its great distance.'

A later historian, the Rev. Joseph Bosworth, wrote of Alfred,

His information was always the best and most accurate, while his opinions and views were ever in advance of his age. Whatever he touched he improved, and left the stamp of his powerful mind upon it. He was noble in heart and thought, as well as action: a king in word, in intellect, and in feeling, - great in mind as well as in station, - he therefore, well deserves the tile universally assigned to him of, KING ALFRED THE GREAT.'

Extracts from King Alfred's Translations

Below is a translation entitled..

'The Description of Europe' done by the learned English King Alfred the Great. During the 9ᵗʰ century. when Leek and it's Lands were ruled over by Anglo Saxon Royalty. King Alfred translated many similar ancient classical works into Old English for the 'instruction and welfare of his people'.

Note the Anglo Saxon letters and fine style of writing.

nupilleþe ymb eupópe land gemære neccan. Spamy cel spaþehit fynmeſt piton; ꝼnam þære ea danaiſ. þær oð ꝛin ꝺaea ꝛeo pylð oꝼþðin beoꝛꝫe. þem an alpiſ hæt. ꝺ ymð þonne noꝛð ꝛyhtæ. onþæꝛ ꝫaꝛ ꝛeꝫeſ eaꝛm. þæþæt land utan ymblið þem an bꝛyttannia hæt. ꝺeꝛtſuð oþ ꝺonua þaea; þære æpylme iſ. neah þære ea ꝛineſ; ꝺiſ ꝛiðꝺan eaſt yꝛꝛenꝺe pið cꝛeca land. ut onþone penꝺel ſæꝫ; ꝺ noꝛð oþþone ꝫaꝛꝛecꝫ. þe man cpenſæ hæt, binnan þæm ſynꝺon maneꝫa ꝺeoꝺa. achitmanhæt eall ꝫeꝛmania; þonne pyð noꝛðan ꝺonua æpylme. ꝺ be eaſtan ꝛine. ſynꝺon eaſt ꝼꝛancan; ꝺ beſuðan

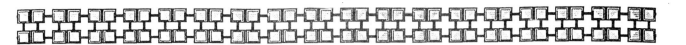

Want to find out more about
ANGLO SAXON ENGLAND?

DA ENGLISCAN GESIPAS

(Old English for 'The English Companions' and pronounced 'The Englishan Yesithas') is the only major historical society devoted to the study of the Anglo-Saxon period. All aspects are covered, including language and literature, archaeology, anthropology, architecture, art, religion, mythology, folklore and material culture.

The society was formed in 1966. Its aims are to increase awareness of the foundations and growth of English culture and to bring together all those with an interest in the period, roughly AD 450 to 1066. It stimulates interest and debate on relevant subjects through the pages of its thrice-yearly periodical, *Widowinde (Anglo Saxon for 'bindweed')*. Membership is open to all with an interest in the period. For details please write to – *The Membership Secretary, Da Engliscan Gesipas, P.O. BM Box 4336, London, WciN 3XX*

THE ENGLISH

ANGLO SAXON

KING HAROLD

Saxon Village

The Saxon Village is a highly innovative educational project producing very accurate reproductions of Anglo-Saxon and Viking artefacts and well designed books for teachers and the rapidly growing number of folk with a keen interest in Anglo-Saxon England. The Saxon Village makes these authentically detailed reproductions available as an integrated resources kit that is specifically designed for the primary school classroom. The kit is affordable without compromising the excellent quality. Most of our products are hand made and finished in the Saxon Village art studio or the workshops of individual craftsfolk within the Saxon Village group. Hundreds of UK schools and tens of thousands of children are now using Saxon Village historical resources kits.

The long term objective of the Saxon Village is to build a dedicated hands-on teaching facility, for all ages and levels of understanding, to explore the nature of Anglo-Saxon life in depth and detail. Sited in the South West of England, it will be an activity based project offering an exciting and colourful new way of learning about the creative life of our distant relatives. If you would like more information on the Saxon Village or have a skill or speciality that you feel would be helpful to the Saxon Village Project, please write today.

Saxon Village
Patron
Tony Robinson
Actor and Presenter
of
Time Team
for Channel 4 TV

Saxon Village Project Wessex
Bradford on Avon, Wiltshire BA15 1QU
Telephone 01225 866663 Fax 01225 867496
Please write clearly and use your post code.
A 1st class stamp will be helpful.

THE CELTIC MYTH.

Many English people today mistakingly mix-up AngloSaxon/Viking culture with that of 'Celtic' culture. However, much of what is written about a celtic culture exisiting in England has no historical or archaeological basis.

Although the Celts of Ireland and Wales did have a form of art qnd mythology, the traditions in England described by some as celtic are totally Anglo Saxon. Strange to say, some of the jewellery being sold in places like Glastonbury is often described as 'celtic'. Sadly, this is a result of ignorance and the mistaken belief that labelling objects in this way somehow gives them an air of mystery. This frequently occurs in publications and books where the author has not done his research properly. On closer inspection the illustrated objects can plainly be seen to be Anglo-Saxon and a visit to the museum where they are preserved would quickly confirm this.

One well-known historian noted recently that, "A great deal of hocus-pocus is talked today about a 'celtic culture. As far as the English are concerned, what we are today we owe totally to our Germanic/AngloSaxon origins".

So, should the shopkeepers of Leek wish to sell Saxon/Viking style jewellery and memorabillia to passing tourists - they can proudly and honestly boast that the objects come from an ancient town which was given its name by Saxon/Viking settlers.

GOLD & GARNET ANGLOSAXON BROOCH WITH 3 BIRDS HEADS.

THE EFFECT OF THE NORMAN INVASION ON LEEK

We have come to the year 1066 AD. Saxon England was by this time the most cultured and richest country in the whole of Christendom. It was a place of learning, great literature, rich tapestries and fine art. Normandy in France on the other hand was poor both in terms of wealth and culture. The French Norman aristocracy looked across at England with envy and greed in their eyes. They liked what they saw and they wanted it for themselves. It was this which led to the Norman invasion of England.

ALMOST EVERYONE HAS HEARD ABOUT THE BATTLE OF HASTINGS IN 1066, THE DEATH OF KING HAROLD AND THE SPECTACULAR VISIT OF HALEY'S COMET. - All of these events were recorded on the famous Bayeux Tapestry.

The people of Leek would have gazed up in awe at the comet - and after hearing about the death of their English King, kept their swords and shields close at hand. At the end of the Anglo-Saxon period it was, 'the right of every Thane to have a 'BURHGEAT' or 'STRONG-HOLD GATE' before his house.

The English armies under King Harold were a formidable fighting force and a match for any foreign army. However, the King was forced to fight two enemies in 1066 - The Norman French and Vikings from Scandinavia, who were in league with the French. Many noble English Saxon warriors willingly laid down their lives defending this country, because they knew what a dangerous, arrogant enemy they were facing. They feared for the lives of the English people, and their fears were to be justified.

In order to justify their attack on this country, the Normans claimed that the invasion of England was a religious Crusade. They said the English King Harold had been put on the throne 'by perjury, a betrayed oath', by an English Archbishop called Stigand who was 'out of favour' with the Pope in Rome. Sadly, when the Normans set sail for England, they did so with the Church of Rome's 'blessing'. The Church, in effect, had no christian right to support such a quest - it was all to do with greed and politics.

So just what kind of people were the French Norman aristocracy who took over England and the Leek Moorlands. - To begin with they were a pretty ruthless bunch. Their ancestors were Norsemen who had originated in Scandanavia. The word

'NORMAN' actually means 'NORTH-MAN'. These invaders had taken over parts of France and intermarried with Frankish princesses. In time they ruled as Dukes of Normandy throughout the 10th and the 11th century. By then they had 'lost' their 'norse-man' identity and become 'French'.

DEDIT: HAROL
ARMA

WHO OWNED THE PARISH OF LEEK IN NORMAN TIMES?

At the time these Norman Dukes began to cast their eyes over England, Leek was an Ancient parish, and it was held in 1066 by the Saxon Earl Algar.

Staffordshire and its Moorlands fell to the invading Normans in 1070 AD. Soon all of England was under a military dictatorship.

In the winter of 1069-70 AD King William, Duke of Normandy, marched his armies across the Pennines heading for Cheshire, where there was terrible devastation. Villages and houses were burnt - men, women, even children were put to the sword - animals were killed, the barns holding food and grain were burnt to the ground.

Once this was done, the Norman King sent for his nephew Hugh Lupus and made him the Earl of Chester in 1071 and also ruler of Leek. However, it was said of Hugh that,

'He wasted his estate and delighted more in falcons and hunting than in the tillers of his land'.

Hugh had two nick-names, Vras - the fat, and Dirgane - the Gross.
He was so fond of eating that in later life he was only able to crawl rather than walk.
He had many sons and daughters, most of which came to a 'sticky end'.
It was recorded in documents that he, 'carried with him not so much a family as an army'.
However, as he grew older he repented of his wasted life and went to be a monk in the Abbey of St. Werburg - But he had only been there three days when he died.

How the people of Leek viewed their new ruler we have no idea, but it's likely they were not well pleased. Hugh was given emergency powers from the King to deal with any trouble that might arise. He wielded these powers shrewdly for his own political gain.

A later Earl who governed Leek was Ranulph de Bricasard. He married Lucia, the daughter of Algar, Saxon Earl of Mercia. He was a peace loving man and looked after his estates in a more civil, kinder way.

It was the powerful Earls of Chester who were to hold the Ancient Parish of Leek until the building of Dieulacres Abbey by the Earl of Chester in later centuries, when it then became Church property.

The Earls of Chester who held Leek were,

Hugh 1 of Avranches (Lupus)	1071 - 1101
Richard	1101 - 1120
Ranulf 1 (Meschines)	1120 - 1129
Ranulf 11 (Gernons)	1129 - 1153
Hugh 11 (Gyffylliog)	1153 - 1181
Ranulf 111 (Blunderville)	1181 - 1232

The fifth Earl of Chester, Hugh, actually died in Leek in the year 1180 AD.

The day-to-day business of the parish was overseen by a Steward or Forrester acting on behalf of the Earl.

Leek and its Moorlands were now part of a Norman colony run by a Norman King under military alien rule. In the early days of the conquest, damage and destruction on a huge scale was the order of day. Many of the Saxon estates in England were confiscated and given over to the Norman knights. However, there is no record of Leek being razed by marauding Norman armies - This may be due to the fact that the town was considered too important a centre - and perhaps the locals were able to 'keep their heads down' until things became more settled - which they did once King William realized that he would have no Kingdom left if he allowed this violent state of affairs to continue.

At one point William Rufus had to call upon the English Saxon Lords to help him keep some of his 'bull-headed' Norman Lords in order. Once the conquest was complete, the King made an effort to adapt to the English Saxon institutions and to set up a genuine Anglo-Norman state.

We have to remember that this conquest was very unlike the previous Saxon invasion. There was no massive influx of settlers - the French took over this country in much the same way as Britain took over India in Victorian times. The only difference being that the Norman aristocracy aquired rich estates, intermarried with Saxon aristocracy and along with the King, stayed here. It is estimated that in the early days of the invasion there were up to 50,000 Normans - mostly soldiers and 2 million English Saxons. However, after a time, 19 people in every 20 were still English Saxon, and they remained the mainstay of the population. The English Saxon language and traditions survived despite the conquest and the French were eventually 'absorbed' by the English.

The French Normans acted in a 'colonial' way and concentrated in centres away from the Saxons. They held official posts such as clerks and administrators. Many positions in the church were handed over to Normans, and in time all of the Bishops were non-Saxon. Despite this, there was no actual concept of Nationhood at that time. This came about much later at the time of Henry the 8th. In those early days, what marked a man out in society was whether he was a Christian or a Heathen.

It was well noted at the time that, unlike their English Saxon counterparts who were called Thanes, the French Knights were 'poor in manners and grace' However, as the years passed and the French aristocrats slowly became Anglicised, this period of history was to become a Romantic time complete with Knights in armour, chivalry, brave Crusaders, long-haired maidens, romanesque churches and massive castles.

It was also a time when kings and Earls with their retinues, Knights, Bishops and holy monks rode and walked along the highways and by-ways of Leek.

LOCAL NORMAN ARISTOCRACY.

After the Conquest much of the land in N. Staffordshire was handed over to the Norman Aristocracy.

Local examples of this hand-over included THE VERDONE FAMILY of ALTON or(Alveton) and their son WILLIAM de IPSTONES of IPSTONES or (Yppenstones)

The Ancient Knights of the Staffordshire Moorlands

Up until the time of the Conquest the Anglo Saxon warriors were called 'Thegns' - these noble English soldiers did not use horses for fighting in battle. However the Normans did - and they also 'adopted' the Old English word 'CNIHT' (Knight), which means youth or warrior, to describe their mounted cavalry. These French Knights often kept large stables of horses, so they needed a great deal of land for grazing and winter fodder. The early Norman kings often took land away from the English Lords and gave it to their own loyal followers.

In the early days, the French Knights were no match for the English Thegns when it came to honour and chivalry. But as time went by these foreign invaders began to see themselves as English, and their manners improved somewhat – England was now their country, France was a alien land across the sea.

Knights on horseback. dressed in all their resplendent finery, would have been a common sight in Leek and the Staffordshire Moorlands. Written records do exist concerning the activities of those early lords who lived here in the 12th century, but we do not have a great deal of information about the Anglo Saxon Earls who owned land before the Conquest. However we do know that prior to 1166 there were five comitial Manors (escheats of Mercian Earls) and sixteen wasted estates which had belonged to Anglo Saxon Lords.

In Anglo Saxon times the Manor of Leek was held by Liafic, Earl of Mercia, who was the famous Lady Godiva's husband - and later, up to the time of the Conquest, by his son Algar. After the Conquest it passed into the hands of a succession of the Earls of Chester.

Betram de Verdon of Alveton (Alton) owned many manors, including the Manor of Ipstones, at around 1086 AD. He 'provided a glove for the King's right hand on the day of his coronation' and supported his arm while he held the sceptre. When he died he was buried at Stone Priory.

His grandson, Bertram also was in possession of the Manor and the castle at Alton. He travelled to Europe to prepare for the King's safe conduct while on a pilgrimage. He also went to Ireland with Prince John and again to Europe with King Richard the First. He was in the Holy lands with the King and witnessed the killing of 5,000 of Saladins men who were executed as a reprisal for killing Christians. He died from a fever in 1192. Bertram will always be remembered as the Founder of the Croxden Abbey of St. Mary, which was built by the Cistercian monks in 1181. His son Nicholas was later buried in the Abbey.

William de Ipstones the First was, according to an undated deed, either the brother or the son of the brother of Bertram. In 1235 William granted to Stephen Abbot of Dieulacres Abbey in Leek, 'free common on all his pasture of Ipstayn (Ipstones) far and near'. William de Ipstones the Second also held Sharpcliffe.

Deeds from the early times mention a great many Lords and Knights who lived in this area - and it seems when they were not fighting for the King they were arranging marriages, making gifts or selling land. For example, John de Ipstones, who was a Knight in 1324, appeared to spend most of his life in 'serious dispute' with the King and the authorities, which caused a lot of local feeling and trouble. At one time he was charged with robbery and breach of the peace. He denied the charge and said he wanted to defend his honour 'with his body' in a dual.

In 1323 the knight, William de Cheddleton was accused of riding 'armed about the Country (with malefactors) to the terror of the people', and of 'insulting the Abbot of Dieulacres' in Leek. He was also accused of stealing a beast from the park of Thomas Furnival of Alvecton.

In 1324 William de Ipstones ejected Thomas de Brumpton from his land and then besieged Brumpton's mother, Mary in her Manor House.

The centuries following the Norman invasion were very turbulent and violent. A Knight with his retainers could hold sway over an area, and the King often had to intervene in disputes over land and property.

However there were, no doubt, many law abiding Knights who rode about the Staffordshire Moorlands doing good and noble deeds - but as is the case today such things often went unrecorded.

Another example is the first BIDDULPH family of BIDDULPH. In 1086 Ricardus Forestarius vel Venator, vel Cheneware, was given the Saxon lands of Biddulph by King William. Richardus's direct descendants, Sir Thomas Biddulph, then later Roger de Biddulph therafter took on the orginal Saxon Place-name of Biddulph. This 'Norman' surname is, even now, uncommon outside the area of N. Staffordshire. The tall, imposing castle-like remains of the original family home, Biddulph Old Hall, still stand today.

Throughout the early centuries Leek and its Moorlands had a good fair share of aristocratic families, each with its own heraldic coat-of- arms. But there are far too many of them to mention here.

LEEK UNDER NORMAN RULE

Under Norman rule Leek became part of a 'FEUDAL SYSTEM'. Although there had been a type of feudal system before, under the Normans it was on a totally different scale. Land was now held in 'FEU' . This meant that every estate was a 'FIEFS', so that all land was held in a chain which started at the top with the King. By the year 1086 every piece of land was owned either by bishops, abbots, earls or the King himself.

Leek was no longer called a Parish but a 'MANOR' . The Manor of Leek had a Lord who was all powerful. The 'Shires' which had existed under the Anglo-Saxons were replaced with 'COMTES' or 'COUNTIES'.

LEEK AND THE 'DOMESDAY' BOOK

The French Normans were experts in bureaucracy, and once Norman rule was established, King William needed to know exactly what he owned. So he sent out his Commissioners to every part of the country. Jurors were then called in from each 'Hundred', which was an area of land, to the Shire Court. These Jurors then had to give an account of all the land that was owned in the 'Hundred'.

Leek was part of 'The Totmonslow Hundred'. This contained quite a number of other Saxon towns, villages and settlements such as Rushton, Rudyard, Warslow, Sheen, Endon, Cheddlton, Grindon, Cauldon, Basford, Alton, Cheadle etc.

The Domesday book was actually written in 1086 AD. It recorded what farming land and forest Leek had back in 1066 while still under the rule of the Saxon Earl Algar.   It reads,

'Rex ten Lec. Algar tenuit Ibi. 1 hida. cu append
Tra. e. X111. car. Ibi funt. xv. uiffi 7 X111. bord cu. vi.
car. Ibi. 111. ac pti. Silus. 111. lenu lg.7 totid lat.
T.R.E. ualb 111, lib. modo. c. folid.

which translated means

King holds Leek (Lec). Algar held
1 hide of land with its dependencies.
Enough land for 12 ploughs.
15 villagers and 13 smallholders with 6 ploughs.
3 acres of meadow
Woodland 4 leagues long and as wide.
The value before 1066 four pounds. After 1066 one hundred shillings.

However, this Norman record does not give a full and accurate picture of the population of the town then. Only those who actually owned land and property were recorded - not their children, relations, dependents, workers, farm labourers - There would have been large, extended family groupings at that time - But we do know Leek had no slaves, as these were recorded in other places such as Uttoxeter. The Norman King was really only interested in the amount of land he held, not in the people who lived there.

Also the Norman French clerks who worked for the King spoke little English and they did not understand the English political structure of land division - The result was they omitted much information, especially in areas such as Leek and its surrounding villages..

Some other places were simply left out, so Leek must have been considered an important place to merit this attention.

The Domesday Book itself is both incomplete and unreliable as a census. Sections of it record only the French residents of an area, while completely ignoring the English Saxon population.

THE FEE OF LEEK

The Fee of Leek was a group of Manors controlled by the Earl of Chester after the Conquest. These manors were administered from headquarters in Leek itself and included Rushton, Longsdon, Ipstones, Waterfall, Calton, Denstone and Hughbridge (*Rushton Spenser*), Le Wall (*'the wall' - later site of Wall Grange, Leek*) and Cheddleton. The Lords of Cheddleton were included because, like the Lords of the other Manors, they owed 'special hunting service to the Lord of Leek (& Leekfrith).

A survey done in the 13th century gives details about a Hunting Ground at Hollinhay, which lay south-west of Leek, near the present day Hollinhay Wood at Longsdon. The Lords of all the estates in the Fee of Leek were responsible for looking after the fencing and they were 'required' to come with their huntsmen to 'beat for stags' when the Lord of Leek had his hunt. Sadly, there are no more magnificent stags or deer now in the woods around Leek – they have been driven out by development and destruction of their habitat.

The area of Hollinhay was part of the Earl of Chester's Hunting Forest of Leek, and they took pleasure in hawking with Sparrow-hawks on Gun and Wetwood. This hunting tradition and the services given by the various Lords to the Lord of Leek existed before the time of the Norman Conquest, and the tradition continued on after 1066. The Estate of Rudyard (Rudegeard) was given in the year 1002, before the conquest, to Burton Abbey by Wulfric Spot. The Royal Manor of Leek was of great importance strategically. It was one of the chain of manors which linked the Earls estates in the East Midlands with the town of Chester – Hence the course of the 'Earl's Way' which ran through Leek.

Earl Hugh the Second issued Charters from his house in Leek in the early 1170's. After his death his son, Ranulph the Third issued Charters there in the year 1210. The Manor of Leek was granted to Dieulacres Abbey in 1232. The Manor had *appendages* – these were areas of land. One of these was Birchall. The 13th century survey gives some interesting details about many of the tenants– For example we are told- *'Richard the Smith gave 12 pence fee or rent to the Earl of Chester, and ploughs and reaps; Adam the clerk paid 18 pence, he ploughs, reaps, carried letters and guards prisoners; Adam of the mill paid 14 pence and ploughed, reaped and gave tallage & ploughshare; Henry the Jew pays 4 pence for the meadow of Ludethok; the 3 bondmen of Wildecroft give 3 shillings and do everything they are ordered to do'.*

When the Normans took over, Leek already had a planned settlement based around the Church and the present Market Place. Most of the suitable farming land had, by then, been well settled over past generations - farming and trade were central to the lives of the people. Under the Normans the THREE FIELD SYSTEM of farming was introduced into the area. This resulted in a regular rotation of crops which in turn gave increased yields.

Old documents tell us that in 1180 the Manor of Leek was selling large amounts of honey and bee-keeping was one of the main local activities.

✠ THE FOUNDING OF DIEULACRES ABBEY IN LEEK ✠

MONKS AND MIRACLES

The following words were carved on a stone wall inside the splendid Abbey which once stood on the fields close to the River Churnet and the present Abbey Green Road in Leek. They read,

'ALAS, HERE IN THE WALL, ENCLOSED BENEATH HARD MARBLE, LIES THE HEART OF THE EARL WHO EXCEEDED ALL IN DARING. O CHRIST THE SON OF GOD IN WHOM ALL THINGS HAVE THEIR BEING, DO NOT SHUT THE SACRED GATES OF HEAVEN TO RANULPH'.

These are sad words, made all the sadder by the fact that the foundations of the Abbey are still there, and along with them perhaps the heart of its founder Ranulph, Earl of Chester. Also the remains of both Ranulph's wife Clemencia, and a great many holy monks must still lie buried beneath the dark earth.

It was recorded, by the monks, that a miracle took place in the 1200's at the tomb of Clemencia. A local blind man recovered his sight after praying there every day.

This site on which the Abbey stood is still Holy and Consecrated ground, and it will continue to be so until the Pope in Rome deems it otherwise. The Revd. Michael J. Fisher, M.A. in his wonderful and comprehensive book on Dieulacres Abbey quoted the following lines;

'For wherever a saint has dwelt..there is holy ground, and the sanctity shall not depart from it....though armies trample over it, though sightseers come with guide books looking over it...'

Through fate of history and later lack of care , the people of Leek have lost so much of their heritage; the slow demise of Dieulacress Abbey must surely count as the greatest loss of all. It was one of the finest Cistercian Monastries in the whole of the British Isles. We need to ask ourselves the following question - Why is the wonderful history of Dieulacres and St. Edward's church not celebrated today in the form of a large, permanent exhibition?

The Tourism Department, the Council and even the Church are failing in their duty by not carrying out this task. Such an exhibition ought to contain photographs, drawings, copies of the many relevent ancient documents plus models of both the Abbey and St. Edward's Church as they were in ancient times.

There was, and amazingly still is, talk by some of building a by-pass through the Dieulacres fields. It is hard to imagine a more sacreligious act in such a holy, historical and beautiful area. Those who really care about the history of our town are often forced to wonder just what is going on in the minds of the people who suggest such ill-judged things. We can only assume they are 'outsiders' who have no real roots here.

HOW DID THE BUILDING OF DIEULACRES ABBEY COME ABOUT?

From the time of the first Earl in the 1100's up until 1214, the Norman Earls of Chester held sway over the everyday fortunes of the people of Leek.

These Earls, to put it simply, were a pretty powerful group of aristocrats. They held territory across the whole of England. One of them, Ranulph the 2nd. had at one time a third of the land of England under his rule. Ranulph the 3rd. who was the Founder of Dieulacres Abbey, was a Crusader Knight at the time of King John and was well noted for his 'noble exploits'.   He had been the sword bearer at the coronation of King Richard the Lionheart.

The story of Dieulacres began in 1206, when the grandson of Ranuph the 2nd. had a dream in which his grandfather told him to send the Cistercian order of monks at Poulton in Cheshire to a new site. We are told that the grandfather's

91

words were,

"Go to Cholpesdale and in a place where has formerly been built a Chapel in honour of the Blessed Virgin, you shall found a Monastry - And it shall be the cause of much joy".

These words, though told in a dream, were wise words - for the monks of Poulton were in great danger from the marauding Welsh, who frequently came over the border into England to plunder holy places and wreak havoc amongst the population.

So, on a warm spring day in 1214 a small group of Cistercian monks and their Abbot, Richard of Poulton, came to Leek and settled on the wide green fields alongside the River Churnet. They would have brought with them many carts containing tools, seeds, food, a few basic altar goods and tents to keep them warm and dry until they were able to construct a permanent stone building. Alongside the carts, walking and trotting, would have come their animals - horses, cows, sheep and the goats. These animals were vital for the monks as they were completely self-sufficient - they produced all their food from their own labours.

The area to which the monks came was at that time called, 'Cholpesdale' and it was part of the estate owned by the Abbey's rich benefactor and Founder, Ranulph de Blundeville, the Earl of Chester

In fact, the Earl actually laid the Foundation stone, and as he did so he is reported to have spoken the Norman French words, "DIEU L'ENCRES" which meant 'MAY GOD PROSPER IT'. From this came the name, 'Dieulacres'.

It was recorded that the Earl gave the monks land,
'BY THE WATER OF LUDDEBECHE, WHICH RUNS BETWEEN RUDYARD AND LEEK AS FAR AS THE HOUSE OF RALPH BEC, AND FROM THENCE TO MEREBROC, AND FROM MEREBROC TO GAVIENDHUL AND DOWN FROM THE HOUSE OF DODI AS FAR AS THE GRAVE OF 'THONI'. FROM THENCE TO FALINGBROC, AND BY FALINGBROC TO FULHE AND FROM FULHE BACK TO LUDDEBECHE'.

The Saxon place-names and watercourses mentioned are still with us today, but most of these Medieval names have changed or developed. For example 'Merebroc' is of course, 'Meerbrook', while the word 'Falingbroc' referred to a brook which ran below the present area of Morridge. The 'Fulche' was a stream between Ashenhurst and Bradnop. Most of this land lay inside the Manor of Leek , but for a while it did not include the town of Leek.

The Abbey's estates in time became enormous and they stretched into three counties - Staffordshire, Cheshire and Lancashire.

The monks were given the patronage of St. Edward's Church along with its dependent small chapels at Ipstones, Cheddleton and Horton. They were also granted the Manor of Leek, and after a short time the actual town itself came under the rule of the Church. The Abbot was then formally allowed to hold a town fair, keep a rabbit warren and attend the Manorial court.

The story of Dieulacres is a fascinating one to say the least. The Abbey attracted close attention from members of the Royal Family, and during its history was visited by Earls, Knights and many other important people.

Dieulacres's history was recorded in;

'THE CHRONICLE OF DIEULACRES ABBEY'

This ancient document was written by 'an anonymous monk' at the beginning of the 15th. century and contains a wealth of information - One section of it starts with the enticing words,

'Here begins a history of the English people'.

There is a description of the British Isles as it was, and notes on the Roman Emperors - It then gives a history of England from the Anglo-Saxon invasions up until the year 1148AD. It also goes into great detail about the later Kings of England and the political intrigue which surrounded them. Much of these writings were done at Dieulacres Abbey itself, for one of the duties of the Leek monks was to read, study, borrow and copy theological and historical works. All the details of the founding of the Abbey and what followed were carefully recorded by a monk from Leek.

93

Abbey Seals.

WHAT THE ABBEY ACTUALLY LOOKED LIKE.

Records tell us that there was already a chapel devoted to Our Lady, the mother of Jesus at the site of Dieulacres before the monks arrived.

The Abbey was built below Hillswood in the valley of the River Churnet. This site was chosen because of the local freshwater supply in the form of springs, streams and the river. The monks dug a well behind the present site of Abbey Farm, only one hundred yards from the Monastery itself - They also sited their 'Fish-pond' at 'Pool-end' where a stream tumbled down from Hillswood. In this pond they kept freshwater fish. We do know from early records that the monks ate salmon.

The Abbey was also granted estates in Lancashire, including the still well-known, 'BLACKPOOL'. The name is an ancient one and literally means 'a black pool', which of course refers to the darkness of the sea-water. In those past times the land was undeveloped and consisted mainly of sand-dunes and flat reed marshes. From this coastal site the Dieulacres monks brought in a regular supply of fresh oysters. No doubt some of these were sold to the people of Leek.

Building work on the Abbey was started in 1214 AD, and the monks quarried local sandstone and a quantity of millstone grit - Alabaster for the altars and chapels was brought in from outside.

As the monks toiled in sunlight and by moonlight, the building that began to rise up above the surrounding verdant fields was both grand and impressive - If we could see it now, we would be over-awed by its sheer beauty, size and magnificence.

The tall church section had a great square tower with a four- sided pointed roof. This held six bells - their musical sound rang out the Benediction across the wooded hills and valleys - The church had small side-chapels, a chapter house and sacristy - stone vaulted roofs, fine stone pillars and arches. Carved figures of angels, saints and Kings decorated the walls. The numerous windows and doors were arched and carved in the Norman style. Within the whole of the Abbey there were eight altars, five of which were made from Alabaster marble.

Within the Abbey buildings there was - 'fine painted glass, Heraldic pavements, finely carved stone-work, many beautiful bosses (carved round stones), gargoyles and statues'.

The Abbey was dedicated to Saint Mary, the Mother of Jesus and to Saint Benedict. The Holy Seal of the Abbot showed a picture of the Virgin Mary with the Christ Child cradled in her arms.

In the working part of the Abbey there was a long extensive dormitory for the monks, an infirmary, parlour, day room, a buttery, larder plus a kitchen in which was kept *'Brass pots'*, *'choppying knives'*, *'chafying dyshys'*, *'hoggesheads'*, & *'various pottes'*.

There were also workbuildings, a brew-house where the monks produced their own ale and cowsheds.

The Cloisters lay on the south side of the building. This was the place where the monks walked and prayed. The cloister was roofed in and glazed, it also contained seats and a **'LAVER'** where the monks could wash before meals.

There were also four elaborately furnished rooms for important visitors. These rooms were called,

'THE RIDERS CHAMBER', 'BUTLERS CHAMBER' and the **'LABOURERS CHAMBERS'.**

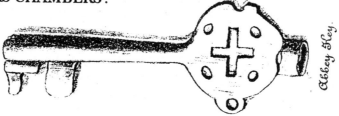

THE LIBRARY was considered the most important room after the church. It had beautifully hand written, illuminated books which are thought to have included,

HENRY OF HUNTINGDON'S CHRONICLE
BEDE'S HISTORIAN ECCLESIASTICA,
HIGDIN'S POLYCHRONICON
OPERA OF GERALD OF WALES
SPECULUM HUMANAE SALVATIONIS
TURRIS SAPIENTIAE

Also kept close to the library were the church vestments 'made of silk and brocade, and woven with gold and silver thread'. The existence of these vestments was recorded at the time, and they included a 'COPE' which was embroidered with Christmas Nativity scenes on the hood section. This cope was draped around the shoulders of the monks when they said the Roman Mass.

An inner-gateway, with a timber-framed arch, gave access to the inside of the Abbey. Outside there was an Inner and Outer courtyard and a graveyard with inscribed gravestones for the monks who died there throughout the centuries, while the Abbots tomb was incised with a cross and a sword. A small scale search by historians carried out on in 1818 unearthed decorated floor tiles and a skeleton. This could well have been the remains of one of the monks. There is no mention of the bones being taken away, so it is likely it was re-buried on the site.

A later inventory gives us an idea of some of the furnishings the monks had. It recorded 'oulde desks', a large silverplated crucifix and 12 candlesticks made from base-metal plus rows of wooden stalls for the monks to sit on. There were oil lamps, three chalices and many altar vessels.

From original records we know that the Abbey had gardens which would have grown culinary and medicinal herbs such as roses, lavender, garlic and fennel. It also had ponds, pastures and fields. Some of these were called,

'FOKERS FELDE, POURS CROFT, BACKHOUSE CROFT, SODENDALE, TWO FOKERS FELDE, PASTURE OF HYLLYSWODE (HILLSWOOD), TH'ABBOTT'S MEDOWS, TH' ABBEY MYLNE, POOLE OF YE MORT, HUNTING GROUNDS, & 'WESTWOOD'.

In fact the Abbey owned land right up to THE ROACHES. On the land they grazed cows, sheep, oxen, good stallions and mares.

THE DAILY LIFE OF THE MONKS.

Life for the monks would seem quite hard today. They were not allowed to wear soft animal skins, furs or shirts but only the roughly-woven monk's habit. They had to retire early to a hard, wooden straw-filled bed, wearing both their tunic and cowl which must have felt very itchy and uncomfortable. Then at midnight the bell was rung so they could go to the church and spend the rest of the night, until the sun rose in the East, 'singing the praises of God and praying'. They were also expected to be give hospitality, and show great kindness and charity, to the poor and the traveller.

The monks could read and write Latin and many were fine craftsmen, gardeners, farmers, scribes and builders. One of the monks would have been skilled in the healing of sick people and animals. They were totally self sufficient.

SIR ÇAWAIN AND THE ÇREEN KNIÇHT

ᗰANY people are familiar with the ancient and wonderful story of SIR ÇAWAIN AND THE ÇREEN KNIÇHT', however some may not be aware that this story is now believed to have been written in the 14th. century by one of the monks at Dieulacres Abbey.

Professor R.W.V. Elliot has pointed out the close similarity of topographical features described in the poem with that of places within the Dieulacre Estates. One of these is Lud-Church, which in the poem becomes 'The Green Chapel'. Lud-Church lies on the northern side of the Estate. It is actually a great chasm within the millstone grit. It is about 200 yards long and its sides rise steeply from 30 to eighty feet high. The chasm however is only 6 to 10 feet wide. The sides are clothed with cool, green ferns and soft moss - the winter sunbeams rarely find there way to the very bottom - When the moon rises it is a magical, mysterious place, full of dancing shadows.

When one reads the poem it is possible to trace the places visited by Sir Gawain. The route of his imaginary journey to th ᕟ Castle of Siir Bertilak de Hautdesert is actually the real route between Poulton Grange and Dieulacres itself.

The following is an extract from the poem 'Sir Gawain and The Green Knight' in which the monk paints a wonderful picture for us of Sir Gawain and his horse, Gryngolet.

SIR ĠAWAYN AND ÞE ĠRENE KNYĠT

BI ÞAT WATZ
ĠRYNĠOLET ĠRAYTH AND ĠURDE WITH A SADEL

ÞHAT ĠLEMED FUL ĠAYLEY WITH MANY ĠOLDE FRENĠES

ÞE BRYDEL BARRED ABOUTE WITH BRYZT ĠOLDE
AND AL WATZ RAYLED ON RED RYCHE ĠOLDE NAYLES

ÞAT ĠLYTEREO AND ĠLENT ASA ĠLEOD OF ÐE SUNNE

ÞENNES HENTES ĠAWAYN ÞE HELME
ÐIT WATZ HYZE ON HIS HEDE HASPED BIHYNDE
WYTH A LYZLLY VRYSOUN OVER ÞE AUENFAYLE
ENBRAWDEN AND BOUNDEN WYTH BEST ĠEMMEZ
ON BRODE SYLKYN BORDE AND BRYDDEZ ON SEMEZ
AS PAPLAYES PAYNTED PERNYNĠ BITWENE
TORTORS AND TRULOFEZ ENTAYLED

Translated this reads

'Then was Gryngolet got ready and girt with a sadle
That gleamed full gayley with many gold fringes.
The bridal barred about with bright gold,
And all was arrayed on red rich gold studs
That glittered and glinted as the gleam of the sun.
Gawain took up the helmet
It was high on his head, fastened with a hasp
With a light embrodied covering on the movable front of the helmet
Decorated and dressed with best gems
On the silken hem and birds
Ornamental stiching
Parrots painted preening between
Turtle doves and true-love knots
So thickly depicted.

The story-teller also gives us a wonderful description of the local moorland landscape-

'Mist drizzled on the moor, Melted on the hills. Each hill had a hat, a huge cloak of mist. Brooks boiled and broke the banks about....

'Sometimes he (Sir Gawain, the Gentle Knight) fought against Worms (Dragons), sometimes against Wolves, sometimes against Trolls of the Forest that lived in the crags. '.. The O.E. word for 'crag' is 'knarre'. This name occurs near to Flash, behind the Roaches.

KNIGHTS The poem contains a great many Scandinavian words, and this reflects the presence and influence of the Viking settlers during Saxon times. It also shows us that the Dieulacres monk may well have spoken English with a Scandinavian dialect. Many of the words contain the hard 'SK' or Viking sound, while the English Saxon words have the softer 'SCH' alternative. The name 'Leek' also took on this 'hard' Viking pronunciation.

The poet had no real need to use these Scandinavian words, he could have used English ones, but in fact poets at that time often used Old Norse words to give emphasis and flow to their poems.

The Dieulacres monk also brought in many Anglo/French elements into his writing, especially describing the fine armour and splendid clothes worn by Sir Gawain.

Although only a poem based on a famous legend, the story of Sir Gawain as written by the Leek monk, gives us a wonderful insight into the customs and life of that time. It allows us see the way our Leek ancestors perceived the world around them.

When the Normans first arrived in 1066, Saxon England was considered to be the most cultured country in the whole of Christendom. It was famous for its beautiful art, sculpture and illuminated manuscripts. A special artistic style existed in these islands called, 'THE WINCHESTER STYLE'. Anglo-Saxon literature and poetry was also greatly admired - however, these centred mainly upon Epics, Heroes and Battles. The hero very often did not live 'happily ever-after'.

The Norman French on the other hand, loved a happy ending. Their literature was full of romance and adventure, in fact very similar to today's romantic novel with its brave heroes and fair damsels in distress. After the 1100's there was a change to this type of poetry and literature. The only problem was that it was written in French, because that was the language of the Norman Aristocracy.

Then, gradually, from the 1300's onwards, a subtle change came about. The King and his Lords began to feel they were more English than French. France was a foreign country across the sea - England was their country. Their children spoke English, the vast majority of the people around them spoke English - Soon it became 'unfashionable' to speak French and not speak English, even within the Royal courts. With this change of language, came a change in literature. Stories were now written in English. And so, the monk at Dieulacres penned his now famous manuscript in the everyday language of the people of Leek.

The poem 'Sir Gawain' tells us some interesting facts about life at that time. For example it talks about . 'CAROLES'. These were a form of dance and song, which existed at the time the monk was writing. These 'caroles' were used at special festivals and were no doubt a familar form of entertainment for the people of Leek.

The festival of 'AL-HAL-DAY' or 'All Saint's Day' on November the 1st. is mentioned too.

The poem also refers to the tradition of giving gifts on the day of New Year. The colour green is also important, as in the 'Green' Knight. This colour was considered to be a magic or fairy colour at the time of Dieulacres Abbey.

The monk carefully describes the weapon held by the Green Knight, which was a combination of a sharp dagger and a battle-axe. He also goes into great detail about the armour worn by Sir Gawain and his horse. Ladies are described as being, 'LOVELY UNDER LINEN' which refers to their beauty and a picture is painted for us in words of a stag-hunt.

CHANGING THE COURSE OF THE CHURNET AND CLEARING THE LAND.

When the monks first arrived the River Churnet wound its way, by a series of 'meanders' across the level flood plain - However in the middle of the 13th. century, the monks straightened the course of the river and pushed back the side of the sandstone valley. This raised the bed of the Churnet in parts by almost eight feet, which posed the threat of flooding in times of heavy rain and snow. To overcome this, embankments were built to hold back the river and an intricate system of drainage channels was constructed to take away all surplus water from the fields.

The monks also built a large, stone-lined water-culvert. This culvert can still be traced today. It runs from the Abbey ruins, towards Broad's Bridge then on to Bridge End.   This was no mean feat, and would have required careful and intelligent planning. They undertook all this work so that they could increase the area of fertile cultivated land for growing crops such as barley and oats, and for grazing their cattle, horses, pigs and sheep.

Because of the danger of flooding, the monks built a causeway across the valley floor. This was called the 'SUREWAY' or the 'SURREY'. We can still see it now, it is the quarter of a mile stretch of road which lies north of the crossing at Broads Bridge which goes on to Abbey Green. It was paved by the monks with stone cobbles. This was later referred to in the 18th. century as the 'SURREY PAVEMENT'.

Much of the land given to the monks by the Earl of Chester was covered in moorland, heath, waste and forest and so a great deal of clearing had to be done to make the land suitable for agriculture.

We also know from records that Dieulacres Abbey had a corn mill sited on the River Churnet. This mill was likely to have already been been in existence before the monks arrived. It would have been a water-driven corn mill, and may well have been situated close to the present site of the James Brindley Water Mill. The monks were allowed to take payment from those who went to have their corn ground there. The Earl of Chester also ordered all his men within the area of Leek to bring their corn to the Mill for grinding. Mill Street derived its name from the presence of this ancient mill.

THE GRANGE SYSTEM

In order to make the best use of the fertile land within the area of the Churnet Valley, the monks set up a series of 'GRANGES' among these were BIRCHALL, MEERBROOK (New Grange), FOKER, WESTWOOD - (SWYTHAMLEY AND ROACH GRANGE). WOODCROFT & FOWLCHURCH (the present-day site of the town's rubbish tip!)

These Granges were actually farms, and were run by what was then called, 'CONVERSI'. These were not professed monks but lay-brethren who, unlike the monks at the abbey, could neither read or write - They also did not join in with the full religious life of the monks - The Nave of the church was the place where they gathered when they did attend services. Their main work was looking after the animals and tilling the land.

Because these 'lay-brothers' did not live according the same strict religious rules as the monks, they sometimes brought Abbeys into disrepute by drunkness and bad behaviour. This reflected badly on the reputation of the good-living monks, and was sometimes used as an excuse to criticise the Holy Church.

THE DIEULACRES WOOL TRADE

In the 1100's the Cistercian order began to sell their surplus wool to merchants from Florence in Italy. When the monks settled in Leek they continued with this trade.

The wool which was sheared from the sheep in Leek was of average quality and so it only fetched between six and ten pounds a sack, unlike the Abbey at Croxden which was selling its wool for eighteen pounds. In a good year Dieulacres could make two hundred pounds from wool. However, each King in turn saw this wool as a source of wealth to supply his armies.

In 1291AD a 'TAXATIO' was introduced which meant that the Leek Abbey had to give the King a certain number of sacks of wool per year. Needless to say, this did not go down well with the monks, for they used the wool to pay off their debts and to cover losses during times of bad harvests, or when their animals fell sick.

King Edward the second expected more than wool from the monks of Leek - He demanded cash. In 1306AD they were obliged to give the King 6 pounds, 14 shillings and 10 pence.

In 1310 AD the King again asked the monks for 40 quarters of wheat, 50 quarters of oats, 60 sheep and 20 oxen .

In 1338 King Edward the third took 6 hundred sacks of wool from the monasteries in Staffordshire, including Dieulacres.

All of this would not have mattered to the monks if the money was used wisely, but it was often wasted on unsuccesful military expeditions into foreign lands. In the monks' eyes, ' the hard-earned fruits of their labours' had been frittered away.

The Ancient Burgesses of Leek

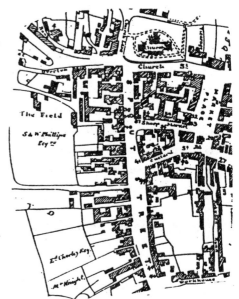

In 1209 Randle the sixth Earl of Chester wrote a Charter which said, *'I will that my burgesses (freemen of Leek) may be as free as the most free burgesses of any borough of Staffordshire'*. Under this charter the 80 Burgesses were each given an acre of farm land, & half an acre by their house; they could use the Earl's forest for firewood and timber and were given grazing rights for their animals on one of the largest commons in England. They were also exempt from paying water-tax. They were not required to pay rent, which amounted to 12p for the first 3 years, and were allowed to freely give or sell their burgages to anyone other than religious. However this ban was modified later, so enabling conveyance to Dieulacres Abbey after 1232. They had the right to choose their own reeve (*magistrate of the town*) and were granted privileged grain grinding at the Earl's water mills. When attending fairs and markets they were exempt from paying tolls throughout the whole of Cheshire.

Ancient town maps indicate that these original land plots, given to the Burgesses of Leek, extended down the West side of the present St. Edward's Street - And may well have extended across to the North side. This suggests that up to eighty 'good' houses existed in that general area in the 13th century.

However, we have to be aware that the building of the 20th century 'Normid' superstore demanded the gouging out of much of the sandstone hill behind St. Edward's Street, including 'Pickwood'. This area formed part of the original ancient Saxon/Norman/Mediaeval settlement centre of Leek. This insensitive act surely led to the destruction of a valuable proportion of Leek's now irreplaceable archaeological/historical remains.

WHEN LEEK BURNT - THE REBUILDING OF THE CHURCH

The Abbot and the monks of Dieulacres were patrons of St. Edward's Church for over 300 years.   When they first arrived in Leek there was already a church on the present site. This would have been the original Saxon church, which was rebuilt by the monks after an accidental fire on June 10th.1297 AD. This fire was recorded in

'The Chronicle of Croxden (Crokysden) Abbey'. by a monk, William de Schepsheved. This Chronicle tells us that not only was the church damaged but also houses, many of which were built of wood and thatch.

A small chapel existed in 'IPSTONES' *(AngloSaxon place name)* at that time, when it was still part of the Parish of Leek. The present church at Ipstones shows evidence of its Saxon origin. Inside the church, are the remains of a large, Anglo Saxon 'TYMPANUM'. This ancient stone carving depicts two intertwined mythical Dragons or beasts with long tails. It would have formed part of the original Ipstones Saxon church.

The rebuilding of the Leek church began in earnest and the work was carried out by local masons and the Abbot's Clerk of works. The Abbot at that time was Robert Burgilon, and it is thought it was he who had the beautiful Wheel Windows put in the church. These extravagant types of window were only usually to be found in great cathedrals and abbeys. It is believed by historians that there were similar windows in Dieulacres Abbey itself.

There was actually something very special about these ancient windows. To the Dieulacres monks, light was a holy thing. They took the biblical words, 'LET THERE BE LIGHT' quite literally. We know that a monastic study of the various properties of light and how they could be used for the glorification of all God's Houses took place in 12th. century France. The builders of Gothic churches used these findings in the crafting of stained glass windows.

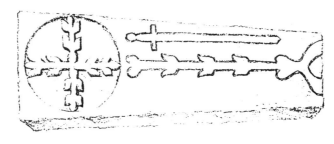

The stone, medieval town church built by the monks of Dieulacres would have been a dark, sombre place without these wonderful structures. We can easily imagine how the people of Leek felt when they saw the wheel windows for the first time. Their own homes were simple, thatched places where only firelight and candle-light lit up the shadowy corners - But as the sun rose over Low-Hill and the dancing prisms of light from the leaded-glass windows filled the church, the town's-people must have thought they were in heaven itself. We take such things very much for granted today, but it is very likely they had never seen anything like it before. Many of them must have stood and gazed in amazement. Little wonder then, that the church was the most important building in the town. It would also have acted as a way-marker for travellers, being easily visible from the high moorlands and surrounding hills.

We also know, from records of the Rev. Loxdale in the 1730's, that there was an Abbot's Chapel in St. Edward's Church which had a carved screen. On this screen was the coat-of-arms of one of the Bishops. This showed two winged creatures which resemble dragons.

In 1838 a map shows the church as still having a 'transept-like projection' at the north-east side of the north aisle, exactly where the wheel-window is today.

Parts of the medieval church still exist today. The West Tower is still the original 14th. century tower, as are the Rose Windows and the North Aisle Windows. Aisles were removed in 1556 and 1593. The columns were originally constructed in a round romanesque medieval style, but unfortunately were made octagonal in 1839. The roof of the church is from the early 1500's and is panelled with carved bosses. The porch was constructed in 1670 and the Archway in 1634.

LEEK MARKET IN MEDIEVAL TIMES.

Leek in medieval times became a thriving Market Town. In 1207 the town was granted a Charter to hold a weekly market and a seven day Fair. This would have merely served as a 'formalisation' of the buying and selling that had been taking place during the previous centuries. After the founding of the Abbey, the Abbot had the 'right and privilege' to take tolls from those who passed through Leek.

On market day the town was full of farmers driving their sheep, pigs and cattle. The dark wooden walls of the thatched houses echoed back the sound of heavy waggons as they trundled into town. Stalls were set up, much as they are today, but the goods on sale were quite different - Live chickens, ducks and geese, piles of freshly grown vegetables, bowls and pots, woven baskets made from reeds, cobblers selling shoes, potions and medicines, herbs and spices from the East and religious talismen claimed to be from the Holy Land were there for the buying or 'barter'.

The Midsummer Fair began three days before the Feast of St. Edward on the 20th. of June and continued for seven full days. When the day of the Fair arrived, people came from far and wide to see the jugglers, cock-fighting, falconry, archery competitions and perhaps a sad dancing bear. Special stalls sold fine silks, ribbons and sweet perfumes in jars and bottles for the ladies. Among the throngs of people were monks from Dieulacres and the rich Lord on horseback with his family and retainers. An Oxen roasted on a spit over a huge fire. The Fair took place at Midsummer when the light and sun were at their best. After the sun had finally dipped behind 'The Cloud' and everyone had marvelled at the double-sunset, then the minstrels begin to play, hundreds of torches were lit and the townspeople danced and celebrated well into the night.

When they tired of dancing the men would go to drink in the inn. This was a simple thatched place where the bare earth or stone paved floor was covered in a deep layer of reeds or dried heather. The only drink available to the ordinary people was the long-brewed mead and ale drunk from wooden cups and bowls.

The colour and pageantry of the Leek Medieval fair must surely have been a wonderful sight to behold. It was a week when everyone wore their best and brightest clothes.

The Ancient Church of St. Edward's – Leek

The beautiful Rose Window

St. Edward's Church stands silhouetted against the sky on one of the most ancient, holiest sites in the town of Leek.

If newspapers had been around at the time of the Leek Midsummer Fair, the report would likely have read as follows:

The Monks of Dieulacres Abbey and the good people of Leek pray for clear weather for the Midsummer Fair.

There is great excitement and activity in the ancient town of Leek, where the good townsfolk are preparing for the popular Midsummer Fair. This is an annual event that begins three days before the holy feast of St. Edward on the 20th day of the mid-summer month of June in the year of our Divine Lord, 1217. All are praying that the sky stays clear so that each may see and wonder at the sight of the double sunset that occurs in the heavens every year.

There are many old ones in the town who tell stories handed down to them from their now long dead ancestors. These stories tell of a ferocious dragon that dwells in the dark earth beneath the present church. It is supposed to guard the treasure of an ancient warrior prince who is buried there. But such stories will not deter the good priest from conducting his Christian ceremony of blessing at the holy fresh water spring that flows from the bank below the church. Young maidens will then deck the spring with sweet smelling flowers and evergreens. and sing the praises of the saints and Our Lady.

Merchants are expected to bring by packhorse and carts goods from every part of England and Christendom, as long as the rain does not fall and the road become impassable. Things to buy will include precious stones, fish, fruit and fine wines. From the exotic East, sweet smelling spices, raisins and currants and shells intricately decorated with pure gold and silver. For the young warrior and archer, well-made swords, bow-staves from Germany, leather-craft and good ironmongery made from Derbyshire lead. For the ladies, there will be rolls of well-woven cloth brought in ships from Flanders, silken threads and delicate coloured glassware. The good monks of Dieulacres Abbey have promised to bring baskets of warm wool taken from their own herd of sheep. Some of the profit they make from their sales will be given to the sick and poor. There will be the usual travelling minstrels, falconry, jugglers, dancing and archery display. Visitors are advised not to set out for the Fair until after sunrise, in order to avoid robbers. Ale, mead, bread, cheese and roast oxen will be served at mid-day.

Great care should be taken not to mistake this original
Medieval 1207AD Midsummer Fair for the later 1629 'Pie Powder' 3 day
Fair.

TRADE & TRAVEL - THE EARL'S WAY.

With the arrival of the Normans, and especially after the founding of the
abbey, travel between Leek and its nearest towns and villages increased. The monks did
not at first do a great deal to improve the roads, but they did build bridges across the
River Churnet where none had been before. However, after 1285 it became the
responsibility of the Leek Abbot to maintain and improve the local roads. The law then
stated that if a road or track became impassable due to its poor condition another track
had to be made alongside it.

The formal establishment of markets in Leek, Alstonfield, Hartington and
oher towns and villages encouraged even more trade. However, care was taken by
those granting the Charters to see that people did not have to travel too far to get to their
nearest market.

In 1256 a medieval lawyer, Henry de Bracton, was employed to
draw up a 'TREATISE ON ENGLISH LAW AND CUSTOM'. This stated that markets had
to have a distance of 20 miles between them. This was declared to be the distance a
person could travel in one day. However after consideration, this was later changed to 7
miles. It was stated that, the journey should be divided into three parts. Part one was the
travelling to market, part two was the time allowed for buying and selling, the third part
was the journey home. It was not deemed safe to travel after darkness because of,
'Ambush and attack from robbers'.

A deed dated 1200 AD from Burton Abbey tells of a '**VIAM COMITIS**' or
'YARLSWAY' or 'THE EARL'S WAY'. In 1313 AD it was called, 'HIGH EARLSWAY'.
This route actually relates to the Norman Earl's of Chester who first held the Manor of
Leek and later helped to found Dieulacres Abbey.

This ancient way marked one of the boundaries of Abbey lands at
'Caldon Grange'. It also followed in part the line of the earlier pre-historic trackway
which passed through the area.

The line runs from Caldon Grange and Waterhouses and follows the line of the Ashbourne Road into Leek via Lower Lady Meadows, Coombes Brook, Gorsthead Mill and Cook's Hollow. You can still see the line of this ancient road in the fields. It is marked out to the east by a hollow and a line of thorn trees. It then passes through Bradnop village and comes out at what was called Pool-hall tollhouse. There was no embankment across the steep-sided valley, so the trackway went down and came up again past the now demolished Lowe Hill tollhouse. It then passed right through Leek and came out north-west of the town. It eventually reached the topographical feature called, 'The Cloud' - Nearby is Earlsway House. After crossing the ridge the ancient road dropped down into the Cheshire Plain.

To help the traveller on his way the road was marked by a medieval cross - Cleulow Cross. This still stands on a high knoll or hill at a height of 1,170 feet above sea-level and would have been visible for miles around. The old way between Leek and Macclesfield via Dane Bridge is quite hilly , but it was still used as late as the 18th. century.

The road was used by the monks when they travelled to the Abbey at Burton. and Combermere Abbey in Cheshire. We also know that the villagers from Waterfall nr. Leek, used it to carry their tithes to Rocester Abbey. The Earl's Way was not really suitable for carts, so long lines of pack-horses were used to transport goods between towns and villages. Carts and waggons needed at least six horses or oxen to pull them, and the wheels quickly became bogged down after rain.

One of the most important goods to be carried along this road was the salt from Cheshire.

Today there is still a by-road running from Abbey Green to Meerbrook. A little way along this route is a farm called, 'Fould'. Close to this farm, a deep hollow-way worn down by centuries of travel, marks the line of an ancient track which climbs up toward the top of Gun Hill. This is a medieval trackway which over time has been called, 'Gun Gate' and 'Trusseway'. It is believed that the monks used this track to carry their wool from the high Granges to Chester. We know from documents that, in the early 13th. century a Florentine merchant was importing 20 sacks of wool every year from Dieulacres Abbey into Italy.

HUNTING IN THE OLD FOREST OF LEKE AND ROYAL VISITORS

In medieval times the county of Staffordshire was noted for the great amount of woodlands, forest and chases it contained. The Domesday Book recorded in the 11th. century that a third of all the county was covered in woodland.

After the Norman invasion the Forest Laws of Normandy were applied to English forests. The word 'forest' itself does not actually mean a collection of trees, but refers to legal rights on land ('the foris') which is not covered by common law. Those who broke the King's Forest Law faced severe penalties. In time the boundaries of these royal forests enclosed villages, towns, farming and grazing land. In the 14th. century the Earls of Chester destroyed many villages and drove away the people in order to expand the acreage of the Royal Forest.

THE OLD FOREST OF 'LEKE'

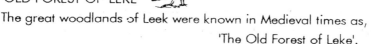

The great woodlands of Leek were known in Medieval times as, 'The Old Forest of Leke'.

'SWTHAMLEY' was a 'Hunting Seat' of the Earls of Chester, and it was described at that time as having, *'Shades and open purlewes and many beasts, hart, hind, buck, doe, wild boar, wolves and grizzly-bears.*

It is hard to believe now that ferocious bears once roamed freely around Leek. As for wolves, it was reported by Sir William de Lacy in 1546 that wolves were still hunting down wild goats in the forest at Swythamley.

Wild Boars had become almost extinct by the 13th, century due to over-hunting, despite the fact that the Boar had been a sacred animal to our Anglo Saxon/Viking ancestors. Local legend tells us that the last wild Boar in England was killed at Wild Boar Clough - Although not quite accurate, this story notes the final demise of the species in this country.

The local population were not so much worried by these wild animals, but by the great number of robbers who hid in the forests and attacked passing travellers. It was a time when every man needed to carry a sword or staff to protect himself, and women never travelled alone.

In 1318 the Leek to Chester road was known and referred to in documents as, 'VIA REGIA' or 'THE KINGS WAY'. This title denotes the fact that part of the Forest of

Leke was considered to be a Royal Hunting Seat used by kings and earls.

It is recorded that King Edward stayed in Leek on the 8th., 9th. and 10th. of August, 1318 AD.

In 1138, an earlier King Edward and the Earl of Lancaster along with two holy Cardinals from Rome, nine English Bishops and many 'magnates from the land of England' , met between Leek and 'Hauthime' in order to exchange 'the Kiss of Peace'.

The Kings had four Royal Forests in Staffordshire. One of these was Macclesfield Forest. No-one but the King himself was allowed to hunt there without permission. However, the main pastime of the medieval upper classes was deer-hunting and they were not afraid to break the King's Law. It was quite common for a Baron or his family to be fined heavily for taking a stag. It was said that when a King died, there followed afterwards a 'great orgy' of deer poaching until the time of the coronation.

There are number of local place-name which reflect hunting activity - these include, 'Wolf-low', 'Wolf-dale', 'Boars-ley (Bosley), 'Stags-hill' and 'Wild Boar Clough'.

The monks of Dieulacres Abbey also hunted regularly and Roger de Menilwarin, the nephew of the Earl of Chester, gave the Abbey 'Free common in his wood of Pevere with husbot (hus = O.E. for 'house') and haybot (O.E. for wood and thorn-trees taken to make or mend wattle fences) as they should have occasion in the presence of his foresters and pannage (grazing on acorns and nuts) for fifty hogs'.

Despite the fact that the Leek monks held a great deal of land themselves, they were still indicted by the King for hunting in his Royal forest. The abbot was accused,
'for that his hounds took 2 stags in the Forest of Makelisfield (Macclesfield) which 2 stags were carried to his Abbey of Dieulacres and there received for use'.

The Abbot was able to defend himself by saying that, it was the previous Abbot who had 'done the deed' and he pleaded with the King not to make him responsible for his predecessor's wrong-doing.

According to the Abbey records the monks kept, 'a magnificent race of great white mastiffs (molossii)'. After the destruction of the Abbey by King Henry the 8th. this breed of dogs seems to have been lost.

We can assume that these huge dogs were kept for hunting - They may also have been used to protect farm-stock, and even the monks themselves, against hungry wolves and angry bears!

When Dieulacres Abbey was founded, the Earl of Chester transferred the title, 'LORD OF THE MANOR' to the Abbot. The Abbot then issued a 'Charter of Liberites' to the people of Leek. Under this charter the townspeople were able to unlease their dogs in the Leke Forest to chase foxes and vermin, but they couldn't harm the deer. They could also gather wild food, dig out peat from the moors for their fires, cut braken and thatch for their houses and also graze their animals after payment of 'pannage' to the Abbot.

However, under the Abbot's charter they were no longer allowed to take timber and firewood from the forest as they had before.

The woodland clearence which began with the founding of the Abbey continued. Trees were felled, brambles, heather and gorse burnt - then a heavy wooden plough pulled by a team of ten oxen turned over the land. Wattle fences were erected and soon level fields and rolling pasture took the place of the alder, oaks, hazels and birch.

All of this must have had quite a devastating effect upon the local wild-life population - It was akin to the modern-day destruction of the Rain-forests in South America - It must also have increased the problem of flooding as the whole eco-system changed. When the rain and snow fell on the surrounding moorlands, there were no trees or substantial vegetation layer to asborb and control the drainage of surface water into the River Churnet and its tributries.

THE FIRST RABBITS IN LEEK.

Rabbits did not exist in Leek, or in the whole of England for that matter, until the arrival of the Normans. They introduced rabbits as a source of table-food.

In 1283, King Edward the 1st. issued to the Abbots of Dieulacres a Royal Charter which read,

'Edward 1, King of England, Lord of Ireland and Duke of Aquitaine directs his archbishops, bishops, abbots, priors, earls, barons, justices, sheriffs, constables, ministers and all bailiffs to allow his well beloved in Christ the Abbot of Dieulacres to have free warren forever within his demesne land of Lach (Leek) and Swythomlee yet provided those lands be not within the limits of our forest of makeselfeld so that no one shall enter those lands to hunt within them or take anything which belongs to the warren without the license of the Lord Abbot and his successors upon forfeiture of 10 pounds. '

The warren is thought to have been sited at 'Westwood Grange' and ancient local field/site-names there reflect this - 'Rabbit Warren', 'Rabbit Burrows' and 'Cunney Greave'. The name 'cunney' is based on the old latin word, 'cuniculus' which means, 'a burrow or a winding underground passage' - 'greave' developed from the Old English word 'graefa' which means a 'brushwood thicket'.

THE BLACK DEATH.

In 1348 'The Plague' or 'Black Death' swept across the land, killing a third of the population. Its coming had been marked earlier by a change in climate which made the weather colder and wetter. This caused bad harvests which in turn led to famine, sickness and unrest. It may have been this which made the population more susceptible to the plague. As crops failed, farmers turned increasingly to sheep-farming.

However, the areas close to the Peak District such as Leek did not apparently suffer as badly as some other areas of the country. The population of Leek, in time, may have increased due to an influx of people from areas that had been affected.

The Chronicles written at Dieulacres only mention the Plague briefly, so it is unlikely the town was severely affected - although it was noted by King Edward, the Black Prince, in 1351 that only a relatively small number of brothers were living then at Dieulacres, which may point to the fact that some monks had died as a result of the Black Death.

VIOLENT TIMES

By the late 1300's there had been a number of changes at Dieulacres Abbey. The Abbey lands were now leased out rather than worked upon by the monks themselves, also the the use of 'Conversi' or the lay-monks had ended in England. The main reason for this was because these monks were causing far too much trouble with drunkness and even crime. On one occasion the lay-monks from Dieulacres were implicated in a murder.

The Leek monks, like most of the other Cistercian monastries in England, had lost all connection with 'The Cistercian Mother House' in France due to the political hostilities that had taken place between the land of England and France. In earlier times the French 'Mother House' would have given guidance and advice, and it would have made sure the monks were living according to the strict rules of the Order. - Now the Dieulacres monks were more or less on their own!

As the year 1400 AD approached, widespread lawlessness broke out in North Staffordshire and in Leek itself. The Abbots of Dieulacres had, by then, become powerful political figures and were often summoned to Parliament - they owned large estates and had many rights and privileges - But this did little to protect them against the general unrest. So the Abbot, like many other members of the upper classes living then, surrounded himself and the monks with a band of armed retainers.

For some reason, feuding broke out in 1370 between a John Warton of Leek and the Abbey. In 1378 Warton, with his own band of armed men, mounted an attack against some of the servants at the abbey and badly injured them. The Abbot tried to bring a lawsuit against John Warton for this violent act, but in the meantime the Abbot's armed retainers, led by Henry and Richard Bradshaw decided that the only way they could get 'justice' for the monks was to take the law into their own hands. They laid an ambush for Warton and his men using bows and arrows. Being outnumberd, Warton had to surrender and he was put into the Abbot's gaol in Leek. After four days he was taken out onto the moors alongside Ashbourne Road and killed.

This may seem terrible to us today, but in fact the Abbey's retainers were behaving no differently from anyone else who lived at that time. Everyone was 'at it' from the King himself downwards. Battles, violence and death were part of everyday life. The retainers believed they were merely doing their duty by defending a holy Abbey and its monks.

However, inquisitions followed and the legal proceedings went on for months. The Abbot, his retainers and even the Vicar of Leek were arrested and imprisoned - but after receiving a pardon from the King himself they were all allowed to escape any punishment.

It would seem the Abbot was liked by the tenants and servants of the Abbey and many people in Leek because they all showed great loyalty to the monks during the troubles.

As the years progressed, things went from bad to worse. The attacks on the Abbey property and servants of the Abbey by lawless bands increased. There were break-ins at the abbey close - trees were cut down, rabbits, hares, pheasants, partridges taken and a great many fish were stolen from the Abbey fishponds. Things became so serious that a Commission of 'OYER ET TERMINER' was set up to investigate matters.

In 1413 servants of William Egerton of Cheddleton broke into houses and the Abbey close at Cheddleton, and cut down many trees there. They then threatened to murder the abbey's terrified servants. This proved too much for one of the monks, Nicholas Poulton - he decided to take the law into his own hands. He gathered together 80 loyal servants from the Abbey lands, who dressed themselves in armour - Then carrying swords and axes they marched from Leek to Egerton's manor house at Cheddleton and took away building stone to the value of 5 pounds, the same value as the timber stolen from the Abbey.

There were both good and bad Abbots at Dieulacres, and for about fifty years during the rest of the 1400's the monks lived a relatively quiet, peaceful and holy life.

By 1500 the Abbey had only a few Granges left. These included Birchall Grange where food was grown for the monastery, Fowlchurch, Westwood and Woodcroft. Other parts of the Abbey estate were leased out by the Abbot, John Newton, to tenants. One of these tenants was called Nicholas Manley who lived at the Manor of Poulton. His lease stipulated that he had to entertain the Abbot from Dieulacres and twelve mounted companions for two weeks in every year and he was expected to dine them on fresh salmon, oysters and wine. Manley was also expected to entertain the Abbot's cellarer and the servants of the Abbey whenever they happened to call.

THE GREAT LEEK RIOT

William Alen was the Abbot of Dieulacres in 1516. In that year there was a full scale riot in Leek and the servant of a man called Paunsfote was killed. Sir John Savage, the Steward of Leek was accused of murdering the servant. Abbot Williams and his servant John Brereton were accused of being involved and in the event, William Egerton from Wall Grange was appointed as the King's Commissioner to investigate the crime and arrest those who were guilty.

But John Brereton was having none of it. There was riot and mayhem as two hundred of the Abbey's servants chased the Commissioner through the streets of Leek from house to house. He was shot at with arrows and finally cornered in a tavern.

Eventually, thinking everyone had gone the Commissioner and his men set off home towards Wall Grange, but they were seen and had to run to St. Edward's Church and take sanctuary inside the bulding for quite a few days. Any of their relations trying to bring them food were sent away. Meanwhile, the roads out of Leek were being barricaded off with trees, ladders and poles to prevent his escape.

The Commissioner did not appear to be harmed, but the Abbot was sent to Fleet Gaol. This incident now seems almost farcical, but it does prove that despite all that had gone on in the past, many people in Leek still liked and respected the Abbot and the monks enough to take up arms and even risk arrrest on their behalf. It also shows that they resented outside interference from the King in the workings of their town.

When Abbot William finally came home to the Abbey in 1519 he found it in a poor state. John Brereton was running the monastery and the monks were just pleasing themselves how they lived. Realising that the Abbot was about to take firm control once more, Brereton and the monks made 'sinister charges' against the Abbot William to the Mother House at Combermere. These charges were believed and he was forced to leave Dieulacres, 'in fear of his life'!

The Abbot appealed to King Henry, who was Patron of Dieulacres. This proved partly successful, but Abbot William never returned to Leek - Instead his place was taken by John Woodland, who 'wasted and spent a large amount of goods of the Abbey'. He was soon followed by the very last Abbot of Dieulacres, Thomas Whitney.

Whitney was no better than his immediate predecessors. Under his rule, trouble continued in the town. He was part of a violent quarrel which took place between a Hugh Willoughby & Hugh Badnall who were on the one side and William Chetwyn & Henry Brooke who were on the opposing side. The argument centred around who owned an area of land at Cheddleton. The Abbot came down on the side of Willoughby and Badnall. An armed band of men tried to evict one of the tenants of Chetwyn. The tenants name was John Massy. The mob went into the farmhouse and threw the children who were inside out of the windows- then all the cattle and animals were driven away.

The Abbot then tried to evict one of his very own tenants, a John Leigh, in Leek. He had all his hedges torn down and his pastures ploughed over. There were many other violent incidences like this including threats, ambush and people being thrown bodily from their houses.

114

Deulacresse Abbey.

THE DESTRUCTION OF DIEULACRES ABBEY.

It is only now, with the gift of hindsight, that we are able to stand back and take a more perspective view of things.

The life of both the Abbey and the people of Leek were closely intertwined with the political and religious events which were taking place in the rest of the England and Europe. We only have to cast our eyes to northern Ireland today to see how a religious divide can cause terrible destruction and unrest within a society.

With King Henry on the throne a growing feeling of unease began to spread throughout the land. Those involved in the church felt unsafe - attacks on monasteries by those who disliked the Pope in Rome were frequent. Dieulacres was especially vunerable because being a Cistercian order they owed a special allegiance to Rome. King Henry had his own ideas on how the Church should be run and about which of God's commandments he wished to obey. He wrongly saw the monasteries as a threat to his authority.   In fact, if he had looked more closely into the matter he would have seen that many of the monks were quite happy to pay respect to the English Church.

The King's solution to his perceived problem went completely over the top. True, there were some bad and unruly monks about, but there were also some extremely good and holy ones - The King, in effect, threw the baby out with the bathwater! - He stripped the monasteries, including Dieulacres, of all they owned and sold the land claiming it belonged to him. This of course was untrue.

The accusation of 'corruption' levelled against the monasteries of England was a pretext for their destruction - And yet, there was corruption in every walk of life, even within the Royal Palace itself. As we all know King Henry was not averse to chopping of his wives heads when it suited his purposes!

The bottom line was, the King had seen the lands and wealth of the church and realized it was all his for the taking. So, in 1537 the attack upon the monasteries began in earnest.

Holy shrines of Saints, where pilgrims had prayed for centuries, were pillaged and destroyed. Priests and monks were turned out of their churches and left with little or nothing. In 1538, Abbot Whitney of Dieulacres wrote a letter to Thomas Cromwell, the King's Vicar General, to plead for the Abbey at Leek. He wrote,

'We have no more churches but one adjoining the monastery, to which belongs no tithes of corn, but oats, and no granges or demesne lands in our own hands, only a few closes to keep our houses and cattle. We beg therefore that such small things as we have may remain in our possession'. **What the Abbot said was true, the monks did by that time have very little – But their pleadings had no effect. The Royal Commissioners came in force from Stafford to take possession of Dieulacres Abbey.**

A SAD END

It was the month of October in 1538 AD. The ancient Anglo-Saxon feast of 'Haerfest' or harvest was drawing to a close. The River Churnet flowed quietly between its green banks, golden leaves hung on the trees and the distant moors were clothed in purple heather.

The great and beautiful Dieulacres buildings stood bathed in late autumn sunshine. No doubt many of the townspeople came to look and to protest against the destruction of their fine Abbey. What did they think, how did they feel as the building was emptied of its contents, the lead removed from the roof, the fine stained glass windows and God's altars were torn out? Did they feel anger and despair rising inside them as the heraldic floors and gravestones were ripped up? Did they shake their heads and sign themselves with the Cross as the last resting places of holy monks, the Earl of Chester and his good wife were defiled?

By the time the sun had set over Westwood, the Abbey had been reduced to almost a ruin. Statues of age-old saints and angels with broken wings stared out onto a scene of desolation and destruction. For the first time in three hundred years, no bells rang out across the green valley, calling the monks to prayer,

It was only later that the truth came out. There were only twelve monks living at Dieulacres at that time, and the serious charges of immorality, which had been levelled against the monks by the King's men, were shown to be totally false. In fact, the Abbey records later showed that the monks were giving shelter to many of the sick and needy inside the Abbey itself - and they were also giving alms to the poor outside in the town and the surrounding area. Who took care of these people once the Abbey had gone, we have no idea. Overall, the monks of Dieulacres probably lived a better and more holy life than many others in the local community - and there is evidence to show that they were still well respected within the town.

116

In the event the sale of goods from the Abbey raised very little money - the grand total was only 63 pounds 14 shillings and 10 pence.   The most valuable items were the altar goods, the lead from the roof and the six bells. These were taken away and never seen again. The Abbey on the day had only 60 lambs, 3 horses, six oxen, 12 pigs, oats, hay and rye.

The Abbot, to his credit, did not take all of this lying down. He out-foxed the King by leasing out some of the Abbey's Estates to his relations and the people of the area. Some of these leases ran to ninety years - by which time the King would be dead!

The Crown attempted to retrieve the leases, but it was not wholly successful..

The Abbot also wrote out blank charters, sealed them and gave them to the former loyal servants of the Abbey after the monastry was destroyed. He claimed no land for himself, the only thing he took with him was the silver-chalice which had been used during the Mass.   There is a similar 'german' chalice today in St. Edward's Church, but it is not thought to be the original chalice saved by Abbot.

The Abbot went to live in a house in Mill-Street.   He actually outlived the King and his son King Edward the 6th. - and he saw the Catholic Mary Tudor come to the throne. His one wish was that Dieulacres Abbey would be rebuilt and he again made Abbot. He passed the silver chalice onto his nephew, Nicholas so that, 'if the monastry of Delencres (Dieulacres) be hereinafter re-edified the said chalice be restored to the said monastry'.

The Abbot never got his wish, but some of the window-tracery, roof bosses, statues of kings and sculptured stone still exist in the farm built at the site of the Abbey. The remains of the foundations and graves lie covered with red earth and wild flowers. Maybe one day something will be done to clear and restore the ruins of this once beautiful Abbey - then perhaps a Holy Mass will be said on the spot where the alabaster high-altar once stood.
That day cannot come soon enough!

If there is life after death, then surely the spirits of the former monks and the Earl himself are there even now, waiting quietly in the shadows for the people of Leek to come once again to that hallowed place.

Be still for the presence of the Lord, the Holy One is here.

The above photograph is the ruined doorway of the Cistercian Croxdon Abbey nr. Cheadle. This abbey was built about the same time as Dieulacres Abbey. Both this and the following photographs show exactly how the Abbey at Leek would have looked just after its terrible destruction in 1538 AD.

The hallowed ruins of Croxden Abbey, nr. Cheadle as they stand today. This is how the beautiful Abbey of Dieulacres would have looked a number of centuries after its sad demise.

................AND THE END

The story of ancient Leek began on the shore of a blue, primeval sea and ended with the destruction of Dieulacres Abbey – for then the age of folk-magic, legend and mystery was passing away. England, along with Europe was moving into a new age, one of so-called enlightenment and discovery. Political, religious and social events were being written down in books and documents.

By 1673 Leek was a 'picture-postcard' town, one full of 'good' houses and thatched cottages. There was a school, various blacksmiths, a carpenters shop, an aromatarin or chemist, a grocers and a number of merchants houses. There were five public houses - the 'Greene-Dragon', 'The White Horse', 'Ye Cocke', 'The George' and 'The Quiet Woman' (White Hart). Leek also held the third most esteemed Market in the county of Staffordshire.

The towns-people still came to the medieval church of St. Edwards to drink from the ancient, holy 'leek' or spring and to marvel at the double, Midsummer sunset from the churchyard, as their ancestors had done thousands of years before -

But all that and what followed is another story.......

ల

'BLAKELOW'

Blakelow, an ancient pagan site, a Saxon grave,
Stands strangely, dark upon the heathery, silent skyline.
A bleak low, a place of winters wild watched over
Now by drifting, speckled curlews,
Their calls haunting, lonely, sad.

But when the moon of Spring lifts silver
Bright above the moorland hills,
They rise, the Saxons,
Once again with rune etched swords,
And helmets, glinting gold,
To stride the paths of honeyed gorse.

Elizabeth Ann Biddulph

('Blakelow is an ancient Anglo-Saxon low or burial mound which stands half a mile from Bottom House, Leek, close to the Ipstones road.)

Bibliography 📖

Place-Names in the Moorlands – *Harry Ball*. Catalogue of the Bateman Collection of Antiquities – *E. Howarth*. Ten Years Diggings – *Thomas Bateman*   The Origins of Beowulf – *Sam Newton* The Peak District – *K.C. Edwards.*. The Story of England's Flora – *Edward Hyams*. Sir Gawain & the Green Knight – *J.R. Tolkien*. Oxford Wordcraft – *Stephen Pollington*   The History of the Countryside – *Oliver Rackham* An introduction to Early English Law. Old English Newsletter (s)– *Medieval Institute Michigan University*. The Handbook of Anglo-Saxon Food – *Ann Hagen*. Spellcraft – by *Kathleen Herbert* The 2nd. Handbook of Anglo-Saxon Food & Drink – *Ann Hagan*. 'WIDOWINDE' – *The English Companions*. The Kings Before the Norman Conquest *Llanerch* .The Domesday Book – *Thomas Hinde* Sources of Anglo-Saxon Literary Culture A trial Version – *Frederick Biggs*. Anglo-Saxon Runes – *J.M. Kemble*. Rudiments of Runelore – *S. Pollington* Dark Age Britain – *Robert Jackson*. English Historical Documents – *Oxford University Press.*The Vikings & their origins – *D. Wilson* Anglo-Saxon England – *Lloyd and Jennifer Laing*. The Anglo-Saxons – *David Wilson* Alfred the Great – *Penguin Clas.*   AngloSaxon Eng. & the Norman Conquest – *H. Loyn*. Anglo Saxon Verse, Charms, Maxims & Heroic Legends. – *L.J. Rodrigues*. Anglo Saxon Riddles. – *J. Porter*. The Concise Oxford Dictionary of English Place Names – *E. Ekwall* .Seeing Roman Britain – *Evans*. The Fall of the Roman Empire – *Michael Grant* The Transformation of the Roman World – *British Free Press*. Tacitus on Britain and Germany – Translation of the 'Agricola' & the 'Germania' *Penguin* .Roman Britain – *I.A. Richmond*. Peakland Roads & Trackways – *A.E.Dodd*. A History of Cheshire – *C.E. Kelsy*. In Search of the Dark Ages – *M. Wood*.   Erdeswick's Survey of Staffordshire – 1844 AD.   Dieulacres Abbey Staffordshire – *Michael J.C. Fisher*. 13th century Earl of Chester's – '*Staffordshire Studies Vol 5*. History of the Parish of Leek – *John Sleigh*. Church Study – *M.M. Penstone* The Tale of Ipstones – *Rev.Brighton* 1937   Rome, Britain & the Anglo Saxons – *Higham* The Spearheads of the AngloSaxon Settlements – *M.J. Swanton* The Archaeology of English – *M. Wakelin*   The Making of the Eng. Landscape – *W Hoskins*. Aspects of AngloSaxon Magic – *B. Griffiths*. The Making of the English Village – *B. Roberts*. Domesday Book – *R. Welldon Finn*. Stone Circles of the Peak – *J. Barnatt*

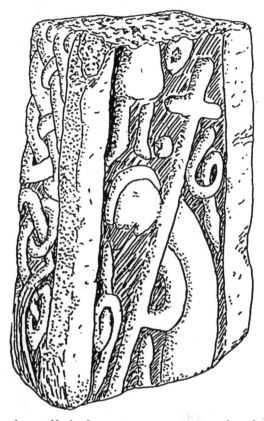

A great many people still fail to appreciate Leek's historical uniqueness. 'Leek's Forgotten Centuries' goes a long way towards addressing this problem. It carefully traces the intriguing history of this very ancient market town through prehistoric, Roman, Anglo-Saxon, Viking, Norman & middle mediaeval times. Drawing upon a wide range of historical and archaeological evidence, it gives a fascinating and stimulating insight into the way Leek people have lived throughout the centuries; their beliefs, language, social structures & customs. The book also carries an ecological and environmental agenda, questioning the destruction and loss of so much of our local countryside, history and archaeological evidence.

'Leek's Forgotten Centuries' also contains extensive detail about local place name origins.

£ 8.95

ISBN 0-9536080-0-X

9 780953 608003